Contents

Pupil Book 5

Unit	1	Dick King-Smith	2
Unit	2	Penelope Lively	5
Unit	3	Funny Verse	8
Unit	4	The BFG	12
Unit	5	The Phantom Sausage Stealer	15
Unit	6	Diaries and Reports	18
Unit	7	Instructions	21
Unit	8	Bears and Lions	24
Unit	9	Classic Stories	27
Unit	10	All Sorts of Poems	30
Unit	11	Fables	34
Unit	12	King Arthur	37
Unit	13	The Adventures of Rama and Sita	40
Unit	14	Fantastical Beasts	43
Unit	15	Theseus and the Minotaur	46
Unit	16	Myths	49
Unit	17	Rain, Thunder and Lightning	52
Unit	18	Bishop Hatto	55
Unit	19	Cautionary Tales	59
Unit	20	Traditional Tales	63
Unit	21	Moonlight and Candlelight	67
Unit	22	Getting Granny's Glasses	70
Unit	23	The Banana Machine	73
Unit	24	Akimbo and the Crocodile Man	76
Unit	25	In My Opinion	79
Unit	26	Riches of the Rainforest	82
Unit	27	Protecting Species	85
Unit	28	Choral Poems	88
Unit	29	Railway Rhythms	91
Unit	30	The Borrowers Afield	94

Dick King-Smith

Dick King-Smith was once a farmer, but is now one of our most popular children's authors. Some of his books are set on farms, and many others feature animals as the main characters.

This is the opening of Dick King-Smith's book Harry's Mad.

Most people walk down stairs, putting one foot more or less carefully in front of the other, and perhaps holding on to the banisters. Not Harry Holdsworth, oh no, not he!

Long hours of practice had made Harry expert in unusual methods of getting from the upper to the ground floor of the Holdsworths' house.

Some were comparatively simple – sliding down the banisters for example, or rolling down the stairs, or hopping down them, feet together, one step at a time. Hopping down but missing out every other step was a good deal more difficult, and could be made harder still by doing it with hands in pockets, or even – the real test – with hands in pockets and eyes shut.

Harry only attempted this last combination when something told him it was going to be a very special sort of day. On this particular morning, something told him.

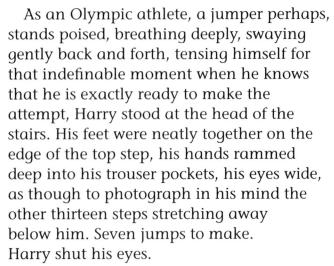

As an Olympic athlete, a jumper perhaps, stands poised, breathing deeply, swaying gently back and forth, tensing himself for that indefinable moment when he knows that he is exactly ready to make the attempt, Harry stood at the head of the stairs. His feet were neatly together on the edge of the top step, his hands rammed deep into his trouser pockets, his eyes wide, as though to photograph in his mind the other thirteen steps stretching away below him. Seven jumps to make. Harry shut his eyes.

He was about halfway down the staircase when suddenly it all happened. Below him he heard his mother's voice calling "Breakfast!" as she came from the kitchen with a loaded tray; behind him he heard his father say "Mind out of the way, Harry, I'm late already," and, right in the middle of Jump Number Five, the postman rang the doorbell, the dog barked madly (as it always did when the doorbell rang), and the cat dashed upstairs (as it always did when the dog barked madly) just in time to receive Jump Number Six on the end of its tail. Jump Number Seven took Harry straight into the breakfast tray.

As the yells of the departing cat and the crash and tinkle of breaking china died away, there reigned for a moment a horrid silence, interrupted only by the slurping of the dog licking up raspberry jam.

From *Harry's Mad* by Dick King-Smith

Harry's Mad

Read the passage, then answer each question.

A Choose the answer that tells what the passage really said. The first one has been done for you.

1. Practice had made Harry an expert in:
   a) walking down stairs b) holding on to the banisters
   c) unusual methods of getting down stairs
   d) putting one foot in front of the other.
   Write your answer like this: 1c

2. That morning Harry:
   a) hopped down stairs, missing every other step
   b) closed his eyes   c) put his hands in his pockets
   d) did all three of the above at the same time.

3. The first thing that happened as Harry was halfway down the stairs was:
   a) the doorbell rang   b) his mother called "Breakfast!"
   c) the dog barked   d) the cat dashed upstairs.

4. Harry:
   a) tripped over the cat b) crashed into the breakfast tray
   c) fell over the dog   d) slipped on some raspberry jam.

B Answer these questions in complete sentences.

1. In what way was Harry different from most people?
2. Why did he wait at the top of the stairs before hopping down?
3. How many steps had he hopped down when he crashed into the breakfast tray?
4. Where were his mother and father when he completed Jump Number Seven?
5. What do you think will happen next? What makes you think so?

C Answer in more than one sentence. What is your opinion of Harry's behaviour? Explain your answer fully.

Direct speech

Today is a special sort of day.

Breakfast is ready

Mind out of the way

Think of **speech marks** as **66** and **99**.

This is a great story

We use **direct speech** when we write the **actual words spoken**.

Father said, "Mind out of the way, Harry, I'm late already."

The spoken words are put inside **speech marks**.

" goes before the first word spoken.

" goes after the last word spoken.

A Complete these sentences with words from the speech bubbles.

1. Harry said, "_____."
2. Mother said, "_____."
3. Father said, "_____."
4. "_____," said the girl.

B Copy these sentences. Put **speech marks** around the spoken words.

1. I'll be home for tea, she promised.
2. Mark said, Let's go for a game of football.
3. What time will you be back? she asked.
4. See who's at the door, called Mum.
5. Will you help me? asked Jan.
6. It's too hot! complained Will.

C Copy these sentences. Put **speech marks** around the spoken words. Add any other punctuation necessary.

1. Pleased to meet you said Jack
2. I've a letter for you said the postman
3. Help cried the man
4. It's ages since we met said Beth
5. Anwar said I've forgotten my pen
6. The water's freezing cried Carlo

D Write five sentences of your own using **direct speech**.

Continuing the story of Harry Holdsworth

Read again the story of Harry and his disastrous attempt to hop downstairs. What do you think might happen next?

Plan and write your continuation of the story.

Paragraph 1: what has happened to Harry?

Paragraph 2: what does everyone do next?

Paragraph 3: what has the postman brought?

Paragraph 4: how does it all end?

Write a different story about Harry Holdsworth.

Direct and reported speech

In **direct speech** we use the actual words of the speaker, putting them inside speech marks.

Farmer Hogget said, "The fair starts at two."

In **reported speech** we say what someone said without using their actual words. We do not use speech marks.

Farmer Hogget said that the fair started at two.

The fair starts at two.

In **reported speech** the **present** tense **changes to** the **past** tense.

'I' changes to 'he' or 'she', unless you are writing about yourself.

A Change these direct speech sentences to **reported speech**. The first one has been done for you.
1. "I'm going to be late," she said.
   She said that she was going to be late.
2. "It's raining again," said Mum.
3. "I'm working hard," he said.
4. "I live near the church," she told him.
5. "I like books by Dick King-Smith," he said.
6. Paul said, "The TV is broken."
7. "English is my favourite subject," said Sam.

B Change these questions into **reported speech**. The first one has been done for you.
1. "What time is it?" he asked.
   He asked what time it was.
2. "Where are you going?" she asked him.
3. "Can you jump over the stream?" he asked her.
4. "Why do you walk so slowly?" Mum asked him.
5. "Is it home time?" he asked.
6. "Who is the fastest runner in the school?" he asked.

C Change these sentences into **direct speech**.
1. Shani said that it was time to go home.
2. Nicky asked if he could go to the park.
3. She asked if anyone had seen her newspaper.
4. He said it was too wet to play outside.
5. He said he was going to buy a new car.
6. She said she was thirsty.

D Write five **reported speech** sentences of your own.

Penelope Lively

Time Trouble

Time Trouble *is an amusing short story by Penelope Lively.*

When I was nine I came to an arrangement with a grandfather clock; it was disastrous. Never trust a clock. Believe me – I know. I'll tell you about it.

I was in the hall of our house, all by myself. Except for the clock. I'd just come in from school. The clock said ten past four. And I said, out loud, because I was fed up and cross as two sticks, "I'd give anything to have this afternoon all over again."

"Would you now," said a voice. "That's interesting."

There was no one there. I swear. Mum was out shopping and my brother Brian was off playing with his mate down the road. The voice came from the clock. I looked it in the eye and it looked back, the way they do. Well, they've got faces, haven't they? Faces look.

"I deal in time, as it happens," the clock went on. "Had some bad time, have you?"

Funny stuff, time. I mean, it can be good or bad, and you're always being told not to lose it and we all spend it and some of us kill it. You can have overtime and half-time and summer time and the time of your life. And there's always next time. And my time's my own, so's yours.

I nodded.

"Sometimes," said the clock, "I can lend a hand." It twitched one, from eleven minutes past four to twelve minutes past. "Tell me all, then."

So I told. About how at dinner I was in a bad mood because of having a fight with Brian and when Mum kept going on at me about something I kept thinking "Oh, shut up!" only unfortunately what was meant to be a think got said out loud accidentally so then Mum was in a very bad mood indeed with me and I got no pudding. And then on the way back to school Brian and I had another fight and my new pencil case got kicked into a puddle and all dirtied over. And we were late and Mrs Harris told us off. And I answered back accidentally and so she sent me to the headmaster and he told me off even more. And I had to stay in at break. And Martin Chalmers nicked my rubber so I had to keep asking for it back so Mrs Harris told me off again.

From *Time Trouble* by Penelope Lively

Time Trouble

Read the passage, then answer each question.

A Choose the answer that tells what the passage really said.
1. Brian was:
   a) the name of the storyteller
   b) the boy who stole his rubber
   c) the storyteller's brother
   d) the name of the grandfather clock.
2. The story began:
   a) when the storyteller had just come in from school
   b) when the clock struck thirteen
   c) at quarter past four   d) all of the above.
3. When the story teller said that time was funny stuff he meant:
   a) it was funny to be spoken to by a clock
   b) the clock was very amusing
   c) the clock was very strange
   d) we use some interesting expressions about time.
4. The afternoon began badly for the storyteller because:
   a) he arrived home late from school
   b) he talked to a grandfather clock
   c) he spoke his thoughts out loud
   d) he had a fight with his brother.

B Answer in complete sentences.
1. Who was in the house when the clock spoke? How can you tell?
2. Explain why the story teller wanted to have the afternoon all over again.
3. What kind of person do you think the the storyteller is? What makes you think so?
4. What did the clock do when it said, "I can lend a hand"?
5. What do you think will happen next? What makes you think so?

C Answer in more than one sentence. Do you think this is a good opening to the story? Give reasons for your answer.

Everyday expressions

Think about these **expressions** from the story:

   a good time   a bad time   killing time
            spending time

Is time really good or bad? How do you kill time? Can time be spent?

There are many everyday expressions which do not mean what they seem to mean.

blow one's trumpet   **rain cats and dogs**
   (to boast)   (rain very heavily)

A Match these **expressions** with their **meanings**.

show a clean pair of heels	not well
get into hot water	a discouraging person
bury the hatchet	run away
throw cold water on	do the best possible
at a loose end	make peace
out of sorts	act without delay
a wet blanket	get into trouble
strike while the iron is hot	discourage
put one's best foot forward	nothing to do

B Use each of the **expressions** in **A** in a sentence of your own to show its meaning.

C Draw an amusing picture for each of these. Say what each expression means.
   a) She has a bee in her bonnet
   b) He leads a dog's life.
   c) He faced the music.

Time Trouble continues

Read the extract from "Time Trouble" again. What do you think the clock will do to help the storyteller? Write your own ending to the story.

- Brainstorm ideas for your story. Make notes.
- Choose your best ideas.
- Plan your story in four paragraphs.
- Write your first draft.
- Edit your work. Is everything in the right order? Have you missed anything out?
- Is there anything which would be better left out? Are there parts which could be improved, or made more interesting?
- Write a second draft, putting everything right.
- Proofread your work. Underline words whose spelling you are not sure of. Check the correct spelling in a dictionary. Circle any punctuation mistakes.
- Write a neat, correct and clear final copy.

Write your own amusing story.
Choose one of these titles.

A Storm in a Teacup
With Flying Colours
Under the Weather

Day 5

Plurals

Most words form their **plurals** by **adding s**:

    drainpipes   cats   birds   windows   gardens

Words ending in **s, sh, ch,** or **x** form their **plurals** by **adding es**:

    bushes   grasses   sandwiches   boxes

A Change these words to **plural**.
1. street   2. brush   3. eye   4. fox   5. sea
6. torch   7. switch   8. church   9. flash   10. bus

B Use each **plural** from **A** in a sentence of your own.

Plurals of words ending in o

Some words ending in **o** add **es** to form their plurals.

    potato potatoes   volcano volcanoes
        mosquito mosquitoes

But other words just add **s**.

    radios   pianos   solos   kilos   zeros
    banjos   photos   memos   dynamos

A Write the **plural** of these words.
1. potato   2. radio   3. volcano
4. cargo   5. tomato   6. piano
7. domino   8. kilo
9. hero   10. video

B Use each **plural** from **A** in a sentence of your own.

Funny Verse

The Silver Fish

While fishing in the blue lagoon,
I caught a lovely silver fish,
And he spoke to me, "My boy," quoth he,
"Please set me free and I'll grant your wish:
A kingdom of wisdom? A palace of gold?
Or all the fancies your mind can hold?"
And I said, "OK", and I set him free,
But he laughed at me as he swam away,
And left me whispering my wish
Into a silent sea.

Today I caught that fish again
(That lovely silver prince of fishes),
And once again he offered me,
If I would only set him free,
Any one of a number of wishes
If I would throw him back to the fishes.
He was delicious.

Shel Silverstein

Ping-Pong

Chitchat	Knickknack	crisscross	singsong
wigwag	geegaw	flip-flop	mishmash
rick rack	riffraff	ding-dong	King Kong
zigzag	seesaw	tiptop	bong.

Eve Merriam

W

The King sent for his wise men all
    To find a rhyme for W;
When they had thought a good long time
But could not think of a single rhyme,
    "I'm sorry," said he, "to trouble you."

James Reeves

League Division Fun

Here are the football results:
League Division Fun
Manchester United won, Manchester City lost
Crystal Palace 2, Buckingham Palace 1

Millwall Leeds nowhere
Wolves 8 A cheese roll and had a cup of tea 2
Aldershot 3 Buffalo Bill shot 2
Evertonill, Liverpools not very well either
Newcastles Heaven Sunderlands a very nice place 2
Ipswich one? You tell me.

Michael Rosen

Rodge Said

Rodge said,
"Teachers – they want it all ways –
You're jumping up and down on a chair
or something
and they grab hold of you and say
'Would you do that sort of thing in your own home?'

"So you say, 'No.'
And they say,
'Well don't do it here then,'

"But if you say, 'Yes, I do it at home.'
they say,
'Well, we don't want that sort of thing
going on here
thank you very much.'

"Teachers – they get you all ways,"
Rodge said.

Michael Rosen

Day 1 — Lots of fun

Read the poems, then answer each question.

A Write the titles of the poems in your answers.
1. Which poems rhyme?
2. Which poem has the most regular rhythm?
3. Which tell stories?
4. Which play with words?
5. Which poem is most like real life?

B Answer in complete sentences.
1. Explain why Rodge thinks teachers "get you all ways".
2. What does the word 'quoth' mean in "The Silver Fish". Why do you think the poet used this word?
3. Explain how the poem "W" uses rhyme for comic effect.
4. Which poem do you like best? Give a reason for your answer.
5. Which poem do you like least? Give a reason for your answer.

C Answer in more than one sentence.

Explain the word play in each line of the second verse of "League Division Fun".

Day 2 — Direct and reported speech

A Change these **direct speech** sentences into **reported speech**.
1. Rodge said, "Teachers get you all ways."
2. "I'm sorry," he said, "to trouble you."
3. The teacher said, "We don't want that sort of thing going on here."
4. "Work quietly," the teacher told the class.
5. "Wait here," the policeman told the woman.
6. "Tidy your room," his mother told Kuldip.

> When changing **direct speech** orders **to reported speech**, use the word **to** in front of the verb.
>
> "Close the door," she told John.
>
> She told John **to** close the door.

B Change these **reported speech** sentences to **direct speech**.
1. She said she liked funny poems.
2. Jonathan told Rodge to sit down.
3. Anita said it was Amran's fault.
4. She told him to open the window.
5. His mother told him to wash his hands.
6. The policeman told the driver to stop.

Handwriting

Copy your favourite poem from page 8 in your best handwriting.

Writing poems

Concrete poems are poems in which the poet arranges his words to make a picture of what he is describing.

Giant Rocket

t
h   o   f
s   a
n   l
o   i
o   n
m   g
A   short.
It bursts
in a shower
of stars
then spirals down
to distant trees,
and ember
d
y
i
n
g

Wes Magee

Waves

Wallo   wa   foll   ea   o
   wing   ves   ow   ch   ther
Billo   cur   sl   bun   toge

th   fl   t   seag   shriek   a   wat
  ere   oats   he   ull   ing,   nd   ches
wh   b   t   netf   gleam   la   cat

Ris   swe   li   an   hea   or   sai
  ing   ll   fts   d   ves   ange   ls
Slid   hu   dri   an   lea   str   trai

You'll have to excuse me.
I must rush off quick.
Writing this poem
Has made me feel seasick.

Jerome Fletcher

PLEASE
DO NOT
MAKE F
UN OF
ME AN
D PLEAS
E DON'T
LAUGH
IT ISNT
EASY T
O WRIT
E A PO
EM ON
THE NE
CK OF
A RUN
NING
GIRA
FFE.

Shel Silverstein

Use some of the poems on page 8 and some of those on this page as ideas for your own poems.

Double word poem

Make a list of double words. Say the words aloud and listen to their sound and rhythm. Choose the best ones for your poem. If you want your poem to rhyme, then match up rhyming pairs.

Here are some double words to start you off: pell mell, hurdy-gurdy, hop-scotch, wigwam, topsy turvy, inside out.

A poem about school

Think of an amusing incident that has really happened at school, or make one up.

Make notes of what happened and what was said. Plan your poem in three or four short verses.

Your poem does not have to rhyme, but rhyming lines in the last verse help to make a more satisfying ending.

A "fishy" poem

Write about a silver fish,
Who kindly offers you a wish,
If you will only set him free
To swim again in the blue sea.
Amazingly your wish comes true.
What did you wish? What did you do?

A concrete poem

With concrete poems, the shape of your poem is just as important as what you say.

First choose a suitable subject. Think of how the words of the poem can be arranged on the page to make a picture of your subject.

Here are some ideas you might use.

- Fireworks: a rocket; a pin-wheel; a Roman candle; a sparkler.

- Small creatures: the path of a butterfly or a bee as it goes from flower to flower; a spider's web; a frog hopping from one lily pad to another.

- A sea poem in which each line is wavy: perhaps getting rougher as the poem goes on, but starting or ending as a dead calm.

- A 'ripple' poem about a stone dropped into a pond: each verse is written as one circle of the ripple. The next verse is a bigger circle around the first, and so on. The beginning of the poem might be the single word "Plop!" in the centre of your poem.

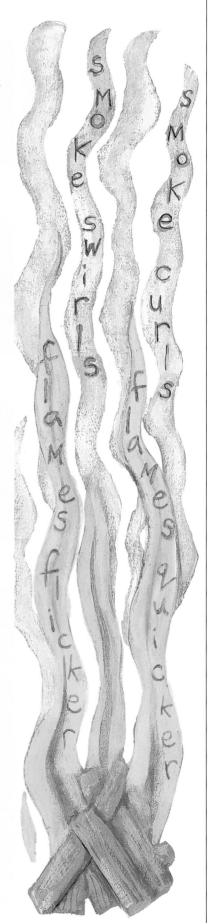

The BFG

This play is adapted from Roald Dahl's The BFG. *The Big Friendly Giant has blown a special dream into the Queen's bedroom window.*

Scene: The Queen's bedroom with a bed and a window.
[*Curtain up. The* QUEEN *is in bed, her crown nearby. It is night-time. After a pause, the* QUEEN's *head tosses from side to side as she dreams*]

QUEEN: [*Talking in her sleep*] Oh no! No! Don't! Someone stop them! Don't let them do it! It's horrible! Please stop them! It's ghastly! No! No! No!
[*As she drifts back to peaceful sleep, a tick-tock sound effect suggests the passing of time, and lighting suggests the coming of dawn. There is a sudden knock on the door.* MARY, *the* QUEEN's *maid, enters carrying a tray with breakfast things and a newspaper*]

MARY: Good morning, Your Majesty. Your early-morning tea.
[*The* QUEEN *wakes up*]

QUEEN: Oh Mary! I've just had the most frightful dream! It was awful!

MARY: Oh, I *am* sorry ma'am. But don't be distressed. You're awake now.

QUEEN: I dreamt, Mary, that girls and boys were being snatched out of their beds at boarding-school and were being eaten by the most ghastly giants!
[MARY *pays attention*]
The giants were putting their arms in through the dormitory windows and plucking the children out with their fingers. It was all so ... *vivid*, Mary. So *real*.

[MARY *has been staring in amazement. The crockery on the tray rattles*]
You mustn't take it so hard, Mary, just because I've had an awful dream.

MARY: That ... that isn't the reason, ma'am ... [*She reaches for the newspaper*] Look, ma'am! Look at the front page! The headlines!

QUEEN: [*Unfolding the newspaper*] Great Scott! [*She reads ...*] "Children vanish mysteriously from boarding-school beds. Bones found underneath dormitory windows!" [*She gasps as she scans the small print*] Oh, how ghastly! It's absolutely frightful! Those *poor* children! Mary! What is it?
[*Suddenly* MARY *drops the tray with a clatter*]
Mary!

MARY: Sorry, Your Majesty ...

QUEEN: I think you'd better sit down at once. You're as white as a sheet.
[MARY *sits on the edge of the bed*]

From *Roald Dahl's The BFG – plays for children* adapted by David Wood

Day 1 — In the Queen's bedroom

Read the playscript, then answer each question.

A Choose the answer which tells what the playscript really says.

1. Dawn is suggested by:
   a) a tick-tock sound effect   b) lighting
   c) a knock at the door   d) all of the above.

2. The queen was woken up by:
   a) a frightful dream   b) Mary
   c) ghastly giants   d) the coming of dawn.

3. The crockery on the tray rattled because Mary realised the queen had dreamt about something that:
   a) had really happened   b) was very frightening
   c) was quite unbelievable   d) was so vivid.

4. The queen told Mary to sit down because Mary:
   a) dropped the tray   b) was as white as a sheet
   c) both **a** and **b**   d) had read the headlines.

B Answer in complete sentences.

1. What sound effects are needed in this play? Why will they be used?
2. What props (furniture and objects for use in the play) are required?
3. What has Mary realised that the Queen has not?
4. How can we tell this from the stage directions?
5. How can we tell it from what she says?

C Answer in more than one sentence. How do Mary's words and reactions help to build up tension?

Day 2 — Adverbs

We can use **adverbs** to describe how people speak.

"Great Scott!' cried the queen **excitedly**.
"Those poor children!" she said **sadly**.
"I think you'd better sit down," she said **gently**.

A Choose a suitable **adverb** from the wordbank to complete these sentences.

> **timidly   angrily
> spitefully   softly   loudly
> sleepily   excitedly**

1. "How dare you!" he said _____.
2. "Don't make a sound," she whispered _____.
3. "Is it time to get up?" she mumbled _____.
4. "It's a goal!" she cried _____.
5. "Where are you going?" he shouted _____.
6. "Is it quite safe?" she asked _____.
7. "No, you can't come with us," she said _____.

B Do the same with these sentences. Choose a suitable **adverb** from the wordbank to complete them.

> **willingly   politely   hoarsely   hopefully
> cheerfully   proudly   happily**

1. "I'm the fastest runner in the school," he announced _____.
2. "I've a very sore throat," he said _____.
3. "We're going on holiday," she said _____.
4. "May I have another ice cream?" she asked _____.
5. "Of course I'll help you," she said _____.
6. "Look on the bright side," he said _____.
7. "May I take your coat, madam?" he asked _____.

C Use these **adverbs** in dialogue sentences of your own.
1. sadly   2. quietly   3. angrily
4. grumpily   5. reluctantly   6. gently   7. politely

Writing a playscript

Continue the playscript of Roald Dahl's *BFG*. What do you think will happen next? Which new characters might you introduce?

● Begin a new line for each speaker.

● Write each speaker's name in capital letters.

● Put brackets around your stage directions,
  e.g. (The QUEEN wakes up).

● Show how the characters react to each other,
  e.g. (MARY pays attention).

● Explain how the words should be spoken, e.g. (She gasps).

● Indicate sound effects and any special lighting,
  e.g. (A tick-tock sound effect suggests the passing of time).

Day 5

Synonyms

Synonyms are words with **similar meanings**.
Synonyms can be found in a thesaurus.

The words underlined in these sentences are all **synonyms** of <u>pick</u>.

She <u>picked</u> a flower from her garden.

The giants <u>plucked</u> the children out with their fingers.

He <u>chose</u> a book from the shelf.

They <u>gathered</u> their belongings.

He was <u>selected</u> for the team.

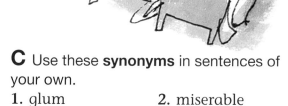

A Choose a suitable **synonym** of <u>caught</u> from the wordbank to complete these sentences.

> **arrested   seized   trapped   snatched
> discovered   came down with**

1. He _____ a cold.
2. He was _____ in the cave by a landslide.
3. He _____ the children hiding in a barn.
4. The eagle _____ the rabbit in its claws.
5. The thief _____ her handbag.
6. He was _____ by the police.

B Sort these **synonyms**, putting the strongest last.
1. delightful, glorious, pleasant, enjoyable
2. happy, overjoyed, satisfied, delighted, pleased
3. cross, sulky, upset, furious, cranky, angry

C Use these **synonyms** in sentences of your own.
1. glum   2. miserable
3. heart-broken   4. bundle
5. bunch   6. clump
7. pretty   8. handsome
9. charming   10. smart

D

1. Find **synonyms** for these words.
   a) cold   b) laugh
   c) strange   d) throw.
2. Use some of the **synonyms** in sentences of your own.

The Phantom Sausage Stealer

This is an extract from Johnny Ball's book The Phantom Sausage Stealer. *In this scene, the sergeant makes a dramatic entrance.*

Cast of characters

SERGEANT TREADHEAVY	a rotund policeman with delicate feet and a red nose
W.P.C. GOLIGHTLY	a bubbly policewoman trying hard to be efficient
DELIVERY BOY	a cheeky Cockney

[*The setting is a police station. W.P.C. GOLIGHTLY is standing behind the counter combing her hair. The telephone rings and she answers it.*]

GOLIGHTLY: Hello, Nutty Street Police Station. W.P.C. Golightly speaking … Who? … Oh, Sergeant Treadheavy is in charge … Speak to him? No … er, yes. He's here … a-abouts.

[*She covers the mouthpiece with her hand and looks off. The phone flex is fully extended and she struggles to get a better view.*]

Oh, where is he? It's important. [*She speaks into the phone again.*] Hold on, he's just coming.

[*She gazes off-stage as if looking through a window and gives a running commentary on SERGEANT TREADHEAVY's arrival.*]

He's crossing the road. He's just coming. [*To herself.*] Come on … Over the zebra crossing and … oh, look out!

[*We hear a crash from the wings and shouts of, "Oy, oy, oy!" SERGEANT TREADHEAVY makes a dramatic entrance seated in the basket of a DELIVERY BOY's bike. The DELIVERY BOY pulls up in front of the counter.*]

TREADHEAVY: Oy, oy, oy! Why don't you ring your bell?

BOY: Because you're sitting on it.

TREADHEAVY: Get me out! Get me out!

[*GOLIGHTLY puts the phone on the counter and tries to pull him out. The BOY also helps but to no avail. Suddenly the BOY gets an idea. GOLIGHTLY steadies the bike while the BOY lifts the back wheel so that the SERGEANT is slowly tilted forward. He comes out with his feet on the floor but stays in a doubled-up position.*]

BOY: Ha ha … a bent copper!

TREADHEAVY: Oooh, me back.

GOLIGHTLY: Can't you straighten up?

TREADHEAVY: No, it's me back, me back.

[*GOLIGHTLY tries to straighten him up, but the BOY again provides the solution.*]

BOY: Try this.

[*He pips the horn on the bike very loudly and the shock straightens up the SERGEANT.*]

TREADHEAVY: Oooh, that's better. Thank goodness.

From *The Phantom Sausage Stealer* by Johnny Ball

Day 1

Enter Sergeant Treadheavy

Read the playscript, then answer each question.

A Choose the answer which tells what the playscript really says.
1. When the play opens Golightly is:
   a) combing her hair   b) looking out of the window
   c) answering the telephone
   d) trying hard to be efficient.
2. The bicycle crashed into Treadheavy:
   a) in the police station b) on a zebra crossing
   c) as he entered the police station
   d) in front of Golightly's counter.
3. The delivery boy called Treadheavy "a bent copper" because the policeman was:
   a) not looking where he was going
   b) sitting in the basket of his bike
   c) a foolish person   d) doubled up on the floor.
4. The delivery boy:
   a) is a cheeky Cockney b) is riding a bicycle
   c) has good ideas   d) all of the above.

B Answer in complete sentences.
1. What is the setting of this play?
2. Find an example of an aside in the playscript. What does it tell us?
3. Who is shouting "Oy, oy, oy" off-stage? How can you be sure?
4. What is meant by "a dramatic entrance"?
5. Explain how Treadheavy came to be doubled up on the floor.

C Answer in more than one sentence. Do you think this is a good opening to the play? Give reasons for your answer.

Day 2

Prefixes

A **prefix** is a **group of letters** added to a word to make a new word.

> **bi-** means *two*,
> e.g. **bi**cycle (two wheels)
>
> **auto-** means *self*,
> e.g. **auto**matic (working by itself)
>
> **trans-** means *across*, *through* or *beyond*,
> e.g. **trans**atlantic (across the Atlantic)
>
> **circum-** means *around*,
> e.g. **circum**ference (the edge around a circle)
>
> **tele-** means *far*,
> e.g. **tele**scope (an instrument for seeing distant things clearly)

A Add one of these **prefixes** to each of the words below.

bi-   auto-   trans-   circum-   tele-

1. graph 2. port   3. phone 4. vision 5. plane 6. cycle
7. stance 8. late   9. text   10. form   11. biography

B Use each of the new words from **A** in a sentence of your own.

C Think about the meaning of the **prefix** in each underlined word and answer these questions in complete sentences.
1. How many languages does a <u>bilingual</u> person speak?
2. What does to <u>circumnavigate</u> the world mean?
3. Whom is an <u>autobiography</u> about?
4. What do you think a <u>telephoto</u> lens is used for?
5. An annual event happens every year. How often would you expect a <u>biennial</u> event to take place?
6. Would you expect light to pass through a <u>translucent</u> substance?
7. How many wings does a <u>biplane</u> have?
8. Would you expect there to be many workers in an <u>automated</u> factory?

Writing a playscript

Continue the playscript of *The Phantom Sausage Stealer*. Why might the delivery boy have come to the police station? What do you think will happen next?

When you have finished your script, get together with some of your classmates to act it out.

Make notes on the script to help you perform it. Think about these things and make notes.

● **Movement:** how the actors will move across the stage.

● **Gesture:** how the actors might use their hands or heads to make their meaning clearer.

● **Delivery:** how slowly, loudly or clearly the lines will need to be spoken so that the audience hears them.

● **Pace:** how quickly or slowly the action takes place; where pauses or silences might help; which words are cues for actors to make their entrances or exits.

Remember!

● Put brackets around your stage directions.

● Show how the characters react to each other.

● Explain how the words should be spoken.

● Indicate sound effects and any special lighting.

S

Day 5

Statements, questions and orders

Statement: You are going to the shop.
Question: Are you going to the shop?
Order: Go to the shop.

A Change these statements into **questions**.
1. It is raining.
2. The library is two miles away.
3. The children are waiting.
4. The film starts at two o'clock.
5. We aren't ready.
6. She will be there tonight.

B Change these statements to **orders**.
1. I am going to bed.
2. You are tidying up your room.
3. She is going to school.
4. I stopped right where I was.
5. He closes the door.
6. She writes neatly.

C Change these questions to **orders**.
1. Are you doing your work?
2. Will you help me do the dishes?
3. Are you hurrying up?
4. Are you speaking clearly?
5. Are you taking a rest?
6. You aren't rushing your work, are you?

D Write three **statements**, three **questions** and three **orders** of your own.

Unit 6

Diaries and Reports

During the Nazi occupation of Amsterdam in the Second World War, Anne Frank and her family hid at the top of an Amsterdam warehouse for two years, while other Jews were rounded up by the SS. Anne began her diary just before they hid away and continued writing until 1 August 1944. Three days later the family was discovered and arrested. Anne died in a concentration camp at the age of 15 in the winter of 1944–45, just months before the end of the war. Her diary was published in 1947.

SATURDAY, 20th JUNE 1942
Writing a diary is a really strange experience for someone like me. Not only because I've never written anything before, but also because it seems to me that later on neither I nor anyone else will be interested in the musings of a thirteen-year-old schoolgirl. Oh well, it doesn't matter. I feel like writing, and I have an even greater need to get all kinds of things off my chest.

WEDNESDAY, 24th JUNE
It's sweltering. Everyone is huffing and puffing, and in this heat I have to walk everywhere. Only now do I realize how pleasant a tram is, but we Jews are no longer allowed to make use of this luxury; our own two feet are good enough for us.

WEDNESDAY, 8th JULY
Margot appeared in the kitchen doorway looking very agitated. "Father has received a call-up notice from the SS," she whispered. "Mother has gone to see Mr van Daan." (Mr van Daan is Father's business partner and a good friend.)

I was stunned. A call-up: everyone knows what that means. Visions of concentration camps and lonely cells rushed through my head. How could we let Father go to such a fate? "Of course he's not going," declared Margot as we waited for Mother in the living-room. "Mother's gone to Mr van Daan to ask whether we can move to our hiding-place tomorrow. The van Daans are going with us. There will be seven of us altogether."

FRIDAY, 21st AUGUST
Now our Secret Annexe has truly become secret. Because so many houses are now being searched for hidden bicycles, Mr Kugler thought it would be better to have a bookcase built in front of the entrance to our hiding place. It swings out on its hinges and opens like a door.

THURSDAY, 1st OCTOBER
Yesterday I had a terrible fright. At eight o'clock the doorbell suddenly rang. All I could think of was that someone was coming to get us, you know who I mean. But I calmed down when everybody swore it must have been either pranksters or the postman.

THURSDAY, 29th OCTOBER
I'm very worried. Father's ill. He's covered with spots and has a high temperature. It looks like measles. Just think, we can't even call a doctor! Mother is making him perspire in hopes of sweating out the fever.

From *The Diary of Anne Frank*

Day 1

Anne Frank's Diary

Read the extracts from the diary, then answer each question.

A Choose the answer which tells what the text really says.

1. Anne's diary was published in:
   a) 1944   b) 1947   c) 1944–45   d) 1942.

2. Anne thought writing a diary was a strange experience because:
   a) she had never written anything before
   b) she did not think anyone would be interested in reading about a thirteen-year-old schoolgirl
   c) she did not think she would want to read it later on either
   d) all of the above.

3. Father's business partner was:
   a) Mr Kugler   b) Mr van Daan
   c) Margot   d) none of the above.

4. A call-up notice meant that father would:
   a) be sent to a concentration camp
   b) no longer be able to use a tram
   c) lose his bicycle
   d) become covered with spots.

5. The entrance of the Secret Annexe:
   a) had a bookcase in front of it
   b) had a secret doorbell
   c) was known only to the postman
   d) was known only to Mr Kugler.

B Answer in complete sentences.

1. In what way has Anne been proved wrong in thinking that no one would be interested in her diary?

2. Who do you think Margot is? What makes you think so?

3. Explain how the Secret Annexe became truly secret.

4. Who was Anne referring to when she wrote "you know who I mean" on the 1st October?

5. Explain why her father's illness was so worrying.

C Answer in more than one sentence. Explain fully why the Frank family had to hide themselves away.

Day 2

A third person account

Diaries help biographers to write the life story of a person. The biographer uses the facts and opinions in the diaries, but changes the first person account into the third person.

Write a third person account of what Anne did, using her diary entries from the 20th June to the 8th July. Begin like this:

On Saturday, 20th June, 1942 Anne Frank began her diary. She found it a strange experience because ...

Recounts

Recounts tell the reader clearly about an event. They may be diaries, newspaper reports, accounts of places visited, or events you have witnessed or taken part in.

Writing your own diary

Write your own diary. Record the things that happen to you, and the events you take part in. Express your opinions and feelings.

Writing a report

Write a report of a recent event such as a sports match, a visit to an interesting place, a school trip, etc.

Use these notes to help you.

● Think about who your audience is, e.g. yourself, someone you know or an unknown reader. Keep your audience in mind as you write.

● Write a short introduction.

● Report the events in the order they happened.

● Link them with words such as **first**, **next**, **once**, **soon after**, **immediately**, **later**.

Writing notes

Many people write their diaries in note form. Rewrite Anne Frank's diary from the 21st August in note form. Begin like this.

FRIDAY, 21st AUGUST
Secret Annexe now truly secret.

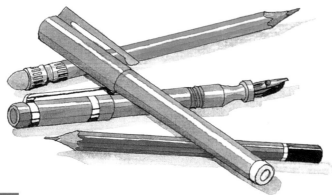

Root words

A **root word** is a word to which a **prefix** or **suffix** may be **added** to make a new word.

cover: uncover   recovery   discover   coverage

press: impress   impressive   express   depress   suppress   pressure

sign: unsigned   design   signature   signal   resign   resignation

port: report   reporter   support   portable   export   import   important

A Copy and complete these sentences. Each of the missing words comes from the **root word port**.
1. This is a very _____ letter.
2. I hope you will _____ me in my campaign.
3. Most of our food is _____ from abroad.
4. He bought a _____ television.
5. He _____ the football match for the *Evening News*.

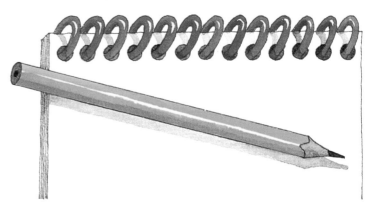

B Copy and complete these sentences. Each of the missing words comes from the **root word sign**.
1. Write your _____ on this sheet.
2. This is my _____ for a poster.
3. Don't do anything until I give the _____.
4. He _____ from his job.
5. The letter was _____.

C Write four sentences of your own using words made from **cover**, and four sentences using words made from **press**.

Instructions

It is most important to follow instructions carefully and to take basic safety precautions, especially when conducting experiments. This experiment is about "dancing" mothballs.

Dancing Mothballs

Mothballs are quite heavy and would sink in most liquids. But in this fizzy combination of acidic and alkaline substances they will "dance" in an amusing way.

Materials
- 5 or 6 small mothballs
- spirit-based felt-tipped pens
- large, glass jar and water
- 10 tablespoons wine vinegar
- 2 teaspoons sodium bicarbonate
- wooden spoon

1. Colour the mothballs with the felt-tipped pens.
2. Add water to the jar until it is three-quarters full.
3. Add the sodium bicarbonate and stir until it dissolves.
4. Add the vinegar and stir.
5. Drop the mothballs into the jar.

At first the mothballs will sink. Then they will dance upward. This happens because the acidic vinegar and alkaline sodium bicarbonate react to make carbon dioxide gas. Bubbles of this gas collect on the mothballs. The gas, being lighter than water, lifts the mothballs to the surface. There the gas escapes, so the mothballs sink again, and the chemical reaction is repeated.

Laboratory procedure
1. Put on old clothes, an overall or an apron before starting.
2. Read through an experiment, then collect the materials listed.
3. Clear a work area and cover it with newspaper or other paper. Put an old wooden chopping board or cork tile on the work area if you have to cut anything.
4. Take care not to get anything in or near your eyes. If this happens, immediately rinse your eyes in clean water, and tell an adult.
5. Never eat or drink anything unless told you may do so in an experiment.
6. Clean up any mess you make.
7. Wash your hands if you have touched a chemical, and when you have finished an experiment.

From *Liquid Magic* by Philip Watson

Dancing Mothballs

Read the passage, then answer the questions.

A These sentences tell you what happened in the dancing mothballs experiment, but they are in the wrong order. Put them into the correct order.

a) The mothballs were dropped into the jar.
b) The jar was filled three-quarters full.
c) As the gas escaped the mothballs sank again.
d) First the mothballs were coloured with felt-tipped pens.
e) Then, as bubbles of gas formed on them they rose to the surface.
f) The vinegar was stirred in.
g) At first the mothballs sank.
h) The sodium bicarbonate was dissolved in the water.

B Answer in complete sentences.

1. What is the purpose of the laboratory procedure?
2. What is the purpose of the dancing mothballs instructions?
3. In which tense and which person are both numbered instructions written?
4. In what ways are the first and last paragraphs in "Dancing Mothballs" different from the numbered instructions?
5. Explain why the mothballs rise.

C Answer in more than one sentence.

Do you think these instructional texts are clear and useful? Explain your answer fully.

Day 2 Making notes

When making notes we write only the important words.

Original text: Mothballs are quite heavy and would sink in most liquids. But in this fizzy combination of acidic and alkaline substances they will "dance" in an amusing way.

Notes: Mothballs quite heavy – would sink in most liquids, but "dance" in fizzy combination of acidic and alkaline substances.

A Write your own notes on the numbered instructions of the mothballs experiment.

B Write your own notes on the explanation for the dancing mothballs.

C Make notes on the laboratory procedure.

- Write only the most important words.
- Use dashes and commas.
- Abbreviate (shorten) suitable words, e.g. write down three-quarters as a fraction instead of words; bicarb for bicarbonate; etc.

Writing instructions

Write your own instructions for making or doing something. Choose one of these ideas, or a subject you know well.

- How to make a paper boat.
- How to make your favourite dish.
- How to find the area of a room.
- How to load a computer.
- How to find an information book in your library.
- How to play noughts and crosses.
- How to maintain a bicycle.
- How to use the Internet.

Organising your instructions

Think about:

- headings
- an introduction
- a list of materials needed
- how you will sequence your instructions
- numbering
- diagrams
- safety warnings.

Checking your work

- Is everything clear and in the right order?
- Have you left anything out?
- Is there anything repeated or unnecessary?
- Test your instructions to make sure they work. To do this carry out your own instructions exactly as you have written them.

Revising

- Are your instructions and diagrams sufficiently clear?
- Make any necessary changes.

Presenting

- Prepare a final draft in your best handwriting and with clear diagrams.

Using notes

A **Without looking back** at the original, use your notes on the mothball experiment to write your own instructions.

B Use your notes on the laboratory procedure to write your own instructions. As you do so, give your own explanation why each instruction is necessary.

C Choose a subject you know well, e.g. a hobby or special interest, as a subject for a two minute talk to the class. Make **notes** on what you will say. Organise your notes into three parts: **introduction**, **main ideas** and **conclusion**.

Unit 8

Bears and Lions

High in the mountain, in a tiny village, an abandoned bear cub is adopted by a lonely orphan child.

Just then we heard shouting in the village square and, glad of any diversion, we all went out to look. Roxanne was staggering towards us, clutching a bear cub in her arms, with its arms wrapped around her neck. She'd been scratched on her face and on her arms, but it didn't seem to bother her. She was laughing and breathless with joy.

"Bruno!" she shouted. "He's called Bruno. I was down by the stream. I was just throwing sticks and I felt something stroking my neck. I turned round and there he was. He patted my shoulder. He's my very own bear, Grandpa. He's all alone. He's hungry. I can keep him, can't I? Please!"

If we hadn't been there – and half the village was there by now – I think the old man might have grabbed the bear cub by the scruff of the neck and taken him right back where he came from.

"Look at him," he said. "He's half starved. He's going to die anyway. And besides, bears are for killing, not keeping. You know how many sheep we lose every year to bears? Dozens, I'm telling you, dozens."

Some people were beginning to agree with him. I looked at Roxanne and saw she was looking at me. Her eyes were filled with tears.

"Maybe" – I was still thinking hard as I spoke – "if you kept him, you know, just for a while. It wouldn't cost much: some waste milk and an old shed somewhere. And just suppose" – I was talking directly to the old man now – "just suppose you made 'bear' labels for your honey jars – you could call it 'Bruno's Honey'. Everyone would hear about it. They'd come from miles around, have a little look at the bear and then buy your honey. You'd make a fortune, I'm sure of it."

I'd said the right thing. Roxanne's grandfather had his beehives all over the mountainside, and everyone knew that he couldn't sell even half the honey he collected. He nodded slowly as the sense of it dawned on him. "All right," he said. "We'll try it. Just for a while, mind."

**From *The Dancing Bear*
by Michael Morpurgo, Collins**

Roxanne's bear

Read the passage, then answer each question.

A Choose the answer which tells what the story really says.

1. Roxanne had found the bear:
   a) in the village square   b) down by the stream
   c) in an old shed   d) near a beehive.

2. At first her grandfather:
   a) was worried that Roxanne's face was scratched
   b) was glad to see that she was safe
   c) was delighted she had found the bear
   d) wanted to get rid of the bear.

3. The narrator suggested that Roxanne's grandfather:
   a) kept the bear to help sell his honey
   b) put the bear in a cage
   c) told everyone about the bear
   d) none of the above.

4. What persuaded the old man to keep the bear was:
   a) Roxanne's tears
   b) the fact that the bear was half-starved
   c) the thought of selling more honey
   d) that all the villagers thought it was a good idea.

B Answer in complete sentences.

1. How did Roxanne's feelings change? Give reasons.
2. Explain why Roxanne's grandfather did not immediately take the bear back where it came from.
3. What do you think was the real reason the narrator persuaded the old man to keep the bear. What makes you think so?
4. Explain fully why the old man decided to keep the bear.
5. What do you think will happen next? What makes you think so?

C Answer in more than one sentence.

What sort of person do you think Roxanne's grandfather is? Explain fully what makes you think so.

Making and using notes

A Imagine you are a newspaper reporter. Make notes for a news report about the bear. You will need answers to these questions.

- Who found the bear?

- Where and how did she find it?

- What did she do?

- How did she feel?

- Why did her grandfather not want to keep it at first?

- What will he do with the bear now?

B Use your notes to write a newspaper report. Think of a good headline. Write your report in four paragraphs.

- **Paragraph 1**: explain where and how the bear was found.

- **Paragraph 2**: explain what happened next.

- **Paragraph 3**: write down what Roxanne's grandfather said when he saw the bear.

- **Paragraph 4**: write down what he intends to do next.

Writing for younger children

Write a new version of the story of Roxanne and the bear cub especially for younger readers.

Audience

- Choose someone to write your story for: perhaps a younger brother or sister, or younger children in your school.

- Which part of the story do you think they will enjoy most? Why?

- Which part might be less interesting? Why?

Planning

- Plan your story so that you concentrate mainly on the most interesting parts.

- Tell the story from Roxanne's point of view. Describe how she felt.

- Use words which younger children will understand and enjoy.

- Make your ending a happy one.

- Illustrate the important parts of your story with two or three pictures.

Verb tense

The **tense** of verbs is often formed by using **auxiliary** (helper) **verbs**.

Past: The lion **was** sniffing at Barry's jeans
Present: The lion **is** sniffing.
Future: The lion **will be** sniffing.

Auxiliary (helper) verbs

Past:	was	were
	has	have
	had	did

| Present: | is | are | am |

| Future: | will | shall |

A Copy and complete each sentence with a suitable **past tense auxiliary verb**.
1. The children ____ walking to school.
2. Barry ___ standing against the wall.
3. He ____ a terrified look on his face.
4. Some children ____ gone into school.
5. Barry thought Tom ____ not have a lion.
6. He ____ closed his eyes.

B Copy and complete each sentence with a suitable **auxiliary verb**.
Write **past**, **present** or **future** for each one.

Do it like this: *He will go to school. (future)*
1. I ____ buying some fruit.
2. They ____ be there.
3. She ____ jogging in the park.
4. He ____ gone pale.
5. The children ____ made a mess.
6. We ____ here.
7. They ____ clean it up.
8. Michael Morpurgo ____ write this book.

C Write six **past tense** sentences of your own, each with a different **auxiliary verb**.

D Write two **future tense** sentences of your own, each with a different **auxiliary verb**.

Unit 9

Classic Stories

E. Nesbit's The Railway Children *is a classic story, read and loved by children down the years.*

They were not railway children to begin with. I don't suppose they had ever thought about the railways except as a means of getting to Maskelyne and Cook's, the Pantomime, Zoological Gardens, and Madame Tussaud's. They were just ordinary suburban children, and they lived with their Father and Mother in an ordinary red-brick-fronted villa, with coloured glass in the front door, a tiled passage that was called a hall, a bathroom with hot and cold water, electric bells, french windows, and a good deal of white paint, and "every modern convenience", as the house-agents say.

There were three of them. Roberta was the eldest. Of course, Mothers never have favourites, but if their Mother *had* a favourite, it might have been Roberta. Next came Peter, who wished to be an Engineer when he grew up; and the youngest was Phyllis, who meant extremely well.

Mother did not spend all her time in paying dull calls to dull ladies and sitting dully at home waiting for dull ladies to pay calls to her. She was almost always there, ready to play with the children, and read to

them, and help them to do their home-lessons. Besides this she used to write stories for them while they were at school, and read them aloud after tea, and she always made up funny pieces of poetry for their birthdays and for other great occasions, such as the christening of the new kittens, or the refurnishing of the doll's house, or the time when they were getting over the mumps.

These three lucky children always had everything they needed: pretty clothes, good fires, a lovely nursery with heaps of toys, and a Mother Goose wall-paper. They had a kind and merry nursemaid, and a dog who was called James, and who was their very own. They also had a Father who was just perfect – never cross, never unjust, and always ready for a game – at least, if at any time he was *not* ready, he always had an excellent reason for it, and explained the reason to the children so interestingly and funnily that they felt sure he couldn't help himself.

You will think that they ought to have been very happy. And so they were, but they did not know *how* happy till the pretty life in Edgecombe Villa was over and done with, and they had to live a very different life indeed.

The dreadful change came quite suddenly.

From *The Railway Children* by E. Nesbit

The Railway Children

Read the passage, then answer each question.

A Choose the answer which tells what the story really says.

1. The youngest of the children was:
   a) Phyllis   b) Roberta   c) Peter   d) James
2. They lived:
   a) at a railway station   b) in Edgecombe Villa
   c) near Madame Tussaud's   d) near a railway line.
3. They were lucky because they had:
   a) everything they needed   b) a perfect father
   c) a mother who was always there for them
   d) all of the above.
4. Their mother:
   a) wrote stories for them   b) visited dull ladies
   c) was never cross
   d) always had an excellent reason for not being
   ready for a game.
5. The characters are presented to the reader through:
   a) dialogue   b) action
   c) description   d) none of the above.

B Answer in complete sentences.

1. What do the words "who meant extremely well" tell us about Phyllis?
2. Do you think the children's mother had a favourite? What makes you think so?
3. Explain why their father was "just perfect".
4. Why do you think the children did not realise how happy they were?
5. What do you think the "dreadful change" might be?

C Answer in more than one sentence.

Would you be interested in reading the rest of this story? Give reasons for your answer.

Adding clauses to sentences

Read these sentences.

We can make these sentences more interesting by adding a **clause**. A clause is a part of a sentence with its own **verb**.

The children were lucky.
You can't go out.

The children were lucky, **because they had everything they needed.**
You can't go out **until you have finished your work.**

A Choose a suitable clause to complete each sentence.

because she hurt her leg
where no one would find him
before you go out
when the car broke down
because it began to rain
when I get back

1. Do your homework.
2. He hid.
3. She couldn't play in the match.
4. They ran for shelter.
5. I'll make the tea.
6. They had to walk.

B Copy and complete these sentences with an interesting clause.

1. He worked hard because . . .
2. They noticed something was wrong when . . .
3. She was popular because . . .
4. Tidy your room before . . .
5. Go and play where . . .
6. We can go to the shops after . . .

C Copy and complete these sentences with an interesting clause.

1. I can't go out until. . .
2. I'll help you if. . .
3. He arrived late so. . .
4. John wrote a letter while. . .
5. He's been afraid of dogs since. . .
6. He finished the work on time though . . .

D Write your own sentences beginning with these words.

1. Because. . .   2. After. . .
3. Although. . .   4. Before. . .
5. While. . .   6. When. . .

Different ways of beginning a story

This picture shows the beginning of a story.
A writer might begin this story in one of three different ways.

● **With dialogue:**
"Help!"
"What was that?" asked Mick?
"Sounds like somebody in trouble," replied Lisa
"Come on," said Chris. "It's coming from the woods!"

● **With action:**
Mick was just about to take the first bite of his sandwich when a sudden cry disturbed the children's picnic. Two wood pigeons, startled by the sound, rose into the air from a nearby wood.

● **With description:**
The grassy bank by the stream was a pleasant spot for a picnic. Close by was a wood which the children intended to explore when they had finished eating.

Write three different opening paragraphs to a story: one beginning with dialogue, one with action and the other with description.

Which do you think works best? Why?

Revise and proofread the opening you prefer.

Add three more paragraphs to complete the story.

Changing sentences

Sometimes we can change the **word order** in a sentence without changing its **meaning**.

Mary was kept out of the way when she was sickly.
When she was sickly, Mary was kept out of the way.

Sometimes a change in the **word order** changes the **meaning**.

The dog bit the man.   The man bit the dog.

A Change the **word order** in these sentences, **keeping the same meaning.**
1. For the first time in my life I felt happy.
2. I found the house straightaway.
3. There was an oak tree in the garden.
4. There was no food left when I arrived.
5. Peter had a model engine for his birthday.
6. You'll be sorry if you do that again.

B Change the **word order** in these sentences so that the **meaning is changed.**
1. The man watched the squirrel.
2. Gareth ran away from his brother.
3. The dog frightened the cat.
4. Jo laughed, but Laila was sad.
5. After he had a swim he went for a cool drink.

Sometimes we can delete words from sentences **without changing** the basic **meaning.**

The man in the blue suit bought a spotted silk tie. The man bought a tie.

C Make these sentences as short as you can **without changing** the basic **meaning.**
1. She bought a new car with air-conditioning and leather seats.
2. The fierce dog chased the frightened man.
3. She bought lots of fruit: bananas, mangoes, oranges and lemons.
4. The girl with the long fair hair lives next door.
5. The lady with the green dress and the white hat is Mick's favourite aunty.

Unit 10

All Sorts of Poems

In the following poems, the poets try to conjure up images by choosing and using words carefully to describe sights and sounds.

Ant

Black is his colour
And he comes out of darkness
To a space of light
Where the grass rattles
And the wind booms.

In his home underground
The stones are silent
Roots and seeds make no noise.

Like fine wires
His legs tremble
Over the ground.
Raindrops hiss and explode
Around him
But he runs zig-zagging
From their cold touch.

At last one raindrop,
Bright balloon of water,
Burst on his back
Becoming his own flood.
Frantic, he spins,
Finds ground again, and scurries
Towards some crack in an
enormous Ark.

Zoë Bailey

What is fog?

Puffs of dragon smoke
Curling round hedges and trees.

Clouds of steam from a giant's kettle
Pouring out over the city.

The breath from a dinosaur's nostrils
Blurring the world into a grey shadow.

John Foster

What is ... the Sun?

The sun is an orange dinghy
    sailing across a calm sea.
It is a gold coin
    dropped down a drain in heaven.
It is a yellow beach ball
    kicked high into the summer sky.
It is a thumb-print
    on a sheet of pale blue paper.
It is the gold top from a milk bottle
    floating on a puddle.

Wes Magee

Word pictures

Read the poems, then write a sentence in your book to answer each question.

A
1. What is the ant doing at the beginning of the poem?
2. What is he doing at the end?
3. What sounds does he hear?
4. List three things that fog is.
5. Explain how the sun is like "a thumb-print on pale blue paper".

B
1. "What is . . . the Sun?" has five pictures. Which picture do you like best? Why?
2. Which picture do you like best in "What is fog?" Why?
3. Explain how a single raindrop is a flood to an ant.
4. What is the "enormous ark" in "Ant"?
5. How does the poem "Ant" make you feel?

C Which poem do you like best? Which lines in that poem do you think are particularly good?
Explain your answers fully.

Similes and metaphors

A **simile** is a word picture which **compares** one thing to another. Similes contain the words **like** or **as**.

The legs of the ant tremble **like** fine wires.
As silent **as** the grave.

A **metaphor** is an unusual and effective way of **describing** something. A simile says something is *like* something else, but a metaphor says a thing *is* something else.

The sun **is** a yellow beach ball.
Fog **is** the breath from a dinosaur's nostrils.

A Copy and complete each of these well-known **similes** with a word from the word bank.

> lion   bee   lightning
> fire   mouse   ice
> peacock   iron   fox

1. as brave as a _____
2. as busy as a _____
3. as quick as _____
4. as proud as a _____
5. as hard as _____
6. as cold as _____
7. as hot as _____
8. as crafty as a _____
9. as timid as a _____

B Find these **metaphors** in the poems on page 30. Write what they are metaphors for.
1. dragon smoke
2. a gold coin
3. an orange dinghy
4. a balloon
5. steam from a giant's kettle
6. a gold milk bottle top

Similes can be changed into metaphors by saying that something *is* something else, instead of *like* it.

C Change each simile in **A** into a metaphor, and use it in a sentence.

Do it like this: *He was a lion on the battlefield.*

Read these poems from India, Japan and the West Indies, then write poems of your own using the ideas on page 33.

Paper Boats

Day by day I float my paper boats one by one down the running stream.

In big black letters I write my name on them and the name of the village where I live.

I hope that someone in some strange land will find them and know who I am.

I load my little boats with shiuli flowers from our garden, and hope that these blooms of the dawn will be carried safely to land in the night.

Rabindranath Tagore (India)

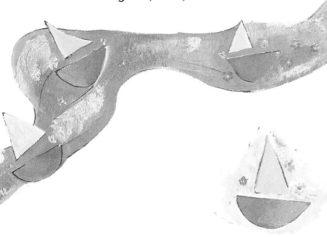

Steel Band Jump Up

I put my ear to the ground,
And I hear the steel-band sound:
Ping pong! Ping pong!
Music deep, rhythm sweet,
I'm dancing tracking the beat;
Like a seashell's ringing song.
Ping pong! Ping pong!
Moving along, moving along,
High and low, up and down.
Ping pong! Ping Pong!
Pan beating singing, round and round,
Ping pong! Ping pong!

**Faustin Charles
(West Indies)**

At the butterflies

At the butterflies
The caged bird gazes longingly,
Watch its eyes!

Issa (Japan)

At Kisagata

At Kisagata
A cherry tree is covered
At times by the waves:
Fishermen must row their boats
Above the cherry blossom.

Matsuo Basho (Japan)

Use some of these ideas for poems of your own.

A metaphor

Write a metaphor poem similar to "**What is fog?**" or "**What is . . . the Sun?**" using one of these subjects: snow, the moon, a cloud, a rainbow, ice, the wind.

Make a list of the things they remind you of, e.g. snow: a blanket, a sheet of paper, icing sugar, an overcoat for a tree, a sparkling carpet under street lights, feathers falling from a pillow in the sky.

Choose your best ideas and use each one in a short verse.

A busy creature

Choose a busy creature such as a bee, butterfly, spider, bird or squirrel. Write a poem about the things they do, and what they remind you of. Brainstorm ideas and use the best ones in your poem. Choose your words carefully.

A haiku

The poem "**At the butterflies**" on page 32 is a haiku. A haiku has just three lines. The first line has 5 syllables, the second has 7 or 8 and the last line 3, 4 or 5.

Choose a subject for your haiku, e.g. an insect, a small animal, the sun, fog, frost, etc. What does it look like? What does it do? How does it make you feel? Choose words carefully to express your feelings and ideas.

A paper aeroplane

Write a poem about a paper aeroplane. Perhaps it has a message written on it? Where will you fly it? How does it fly? What does it remind you of? How does it make you feel?

Music

Write a poem about a musical instrument, or a type of music you enjoy. What does it sound like? What rhythm does it have? How does it make you feel? Include all these ideas in your poem.

Fables

In the sixth century BC Aesop wrote many fables – short stories which usually have animals as the main characters and which teach a moral.

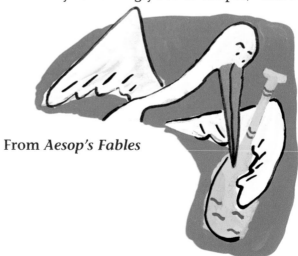

The Dove and the Ant

An Ant was speeding along on its three pair of legs when suddenly, it stopped.

"I'm thirsty," the Ant said aloud.

"Why don't you get a drink of water from the brook?" cooed a Dove perched in a nearby tree. "The brook is close by. Just be careful you don't fall in."

The Ant sped to the brook and began to drink.

A sudden wind blew the Ant into the water.

"Help!" the Ant cried, "I'm drowning!"

The Dove knew it had to act quickly to save the Ant. With its beak, the Dove broke a twig from the tree.
Then, the Dove flew over the brook with the twig and dropped it to the Ant.

The Ant climbed onto the twig and floated ashore.

Not long afterward, the Ant saw a Hunter. He was setting a trap to catch the Dove.

The Dove began to fly toward the trap.

The Ant knew it had to act quickly to save the Dove.

The Ant opened its strong jaws and bit the bare ankle of the Hunter.

"Ouch!" the Hunter cried.

The Dove heard the Hunter and flew away.

The Fox and the Stork

A stork, who had just arrived from another country, was invited to dinner by a fox. The stork was delighted to be asked and went to the fox's home, feeling good and hungry. When she got there she discovered that the fox had prepared some clear soup and served it up in dishes that were so shallow she could not get her long beak in. She had to watch her host while he tucked in, and when he had finished, she went home, still hungry.

Next day the stork invited the fox to dine with her. The fox accepted the invitation, but when he arrived he found that she had prepared some thick soup which she served in tall jars. She stuck in her beak and really enjoyed her meal while the fox, almost fainting with hunger and unable to get his snout in, had to sit and watch.

When she had finished she smiled at him. "I'm only following your example," she said.

From *Aesop's Fables*

Day 1 Aesop's fables

Read the fables, then answer each question.

A Choose the answer which tells what the fables really say.

1. The ant:
   a) fell into the brook b) was blown into the brook
   c) was pushed into the brook
   d) hid in the brook from the hunter.
2. The dove:
   a) picked up the ant in its beak b) saw a hunter
   c) set a trap to catch the ant
   d) dropped a twig into the brook.
3. The ant bit:
   a) the dove to make it fly away
   b) the hunter to make him run away
   c) the hunter so that his cry would warn the dove
   d) none of the above.
4. The fox:
   a) served soup in shallow bowls b) served soup in tall jars
   c) followed the stork's example
   d) had just arrived from a foreign country.
5. The stork:
   a) taught the fox a lesson b) served thick soup in tall jars
   c) was delighted to be asked to the fox's home
   d) all of the above.

B Answer in complete sentences.

1. Explain how the ant saved the dove.
2. Explain why the fox could not eat the stork's soup.
3. How do you think the fox felt at the end of the story?
4. Which fable do you like best? Give a reason for your answer.
5. Why do you think Aesop told these stories?

C Answer in more than one sentence.

What is the moral of each fable?

Explain your answers fully.

Day 2 Words which sound like their meaning

Some words sound like their meaning.

A Copy and complete these sentences with a suitable word from the wordbank.

> **tick twang rat-tat-tat**
> **cuckoo quack bang**

1. I lay awake, listening to the _____ of the clock.
2. He was startled by a _____ at the door.
3. A loud _____ told her she was near the pond.
4. The sound of the _____ can be heard in spring.
5. There was a loud _____ as the gun went off.
6. The bow string went ___ as she fired the arrow.

B Complete each sentence with a suitable word of your own.

1. The cork came out of the bottle with a loud ___.
2. The steam ____.
3. There was a sudden ____ of thunder.
4. The ___ of the tap began to annoy her.
5. The metal rod fell with a _____.
6. He could hear the ___ of bees, the ___ of birds and the ____ of a brook.

C Put each word in a sentence of your own to show its meaning.

1. splash 2. clang 3. gurgle 4. jingle 5. boom
6. rustle 7. neigh 8. toot 9. cluck 10. trickle

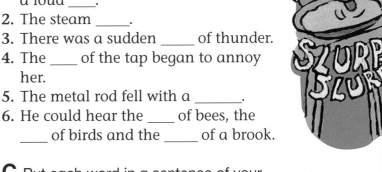

Writing your own fable

A **fable** is a short story which teaches a **moral** lesson, usually with animal characters.

Use the ideas below to help you write your own fable.

> A **proverb** is a traditional short sentence which gives **advice**, or makes a **comment** about life.

Choose one of these proverbs as the moral for your fable.

- One good turn deserves another.
- Every dog has its day.
- He who laughs last, laughs longest.
- Leave well alone.
- Once bitten twice shy.
- Pride goes before a fall.
- Where there's a will there's a way.
- Look before you leap.

- Choose a moral for your fable.
- Choose suitable animal characters.
- Make up a story about them which will teach the moral.
- Look at how fables begin and end. Start and end your fable in a similar way.

Spelling rules

> There is a spelling rule for adding **full** as a suffix.
> **use**: The wild pigeons gave the caged pigeon **useful** advice.
> **success**: It was **successful** in escaping from its cage.
> **wonder**: Being free was **wonderful**.

A Can you work out the spelling rule for adding **full** as a suffix? Write the rule.

B Add the suffix **full** to these words. Use each word in a sentence of your own.
1. thought 2. help 3. care 4. hope
5. play 6. tear 7. faith 8. dread

> Adding -**ed**, -**ing** or -**er**:
> **hum**: She **hummed** quietly to herself.
> **clap**: The audience is **clapping**.
> **fit**: He is much **fitter** than he was.

A Can you work out the spelling rule for adding a suffix to single syllable words which end in a single consonant? Write the rule.

B Add -**ing**, -**ed** or -**er** to these words. Use each one in a sentence of your own.
1. wet 2. sit 3. fat 4. bat 5. drop
6. slip 7. run 8. rub 9. stop 10. sip

Unit 12

King Arthur

This tale is from the legend of King Arthur. A legend is a story about a heroic character. Legends may be based on truth, but change in the retelling and often there are many different versions of the same story.

Without stopping to read what was written on the stone, Arthur pulled out the sword at a touch, ran back to his horse, and in a few minutes had caught up with Sir Kay and handed it over to him.

Arthur knew nothing of what sword it was, but Kay had already tried to pull it from the anvil, and saw at a glance that it was the same one. Instantly he rode to his father Sir Ector, and said:

"Sir! Look, here is the sword out of the stone! So you see I must be the true-born King of all Britain!"

But Sir Ector knew better than to believe Sir Kay too readily. Instead he rode back with him to the church, and there made him swear a solemn oath with his hands on the Bible to say truly how he came by the sword.

"My brother Arthur brought it to me," said Kay, with a sigh.

"And how did *you* get the sword?" asked Sir Ector.

"Sir, I will tell you," said Arthur, fearing that he had done wrong. "Kay sent me to fetch his sword, but I could not come to it. Then I remembered having seen this sword sticking uselessly into an anvil in the churchyard. I thought it could be put to a better use in my brother's hand – so I fetched it."

"Did you find no knights guarding the sword?" asked Sir Ector.

"Never a one," said Arthur.

"Well, put the sword back into the anvil, and let us see you draw it out," commanded Sir Ector.

"That's easily done," said Arthur, puzzled by all this trouble over a sword, and he set it back easily into the anvil.

Then Sir Kay seized it by the hilt and pulled his hardest: but struggle and strain as he might, he could not move it by a hair's breadth. Sir Ector tried also, but with no better success.

"Pull it out," he said to Arthur.

And Arthur, more and more bewildered, put his hand to the hilt and drew forth the sword as if out of a well-greased scabbard.

"Now," said Sir Ector, kneeling before Arthur and bowing his head in reverence, "I understand that you and none other are the true-born King of this land."

"Why? Oh why is it I? Why do you kneel to me, my father?" cried Arthur.

"It is God's will that whoso might draw forth the sword out of the stone and out of the anvil is the true-born King of Britain," said Sir Ector.

From *King Arthur and his Knights of the Round Table* retold by Roger Lancelyn Green

The sword in the anvil

Read the passage, then answer each question.

A Choose the answer which tells what the legend really says.

1. Arthur:
   a) read what was written on the stone
   b) pulled out the sword without reading the stone
   c) could not understand what was written on the stone
   d) none of the above.

2. When Sir Kay swore a solemn oath he said that:
   a) he must be the true-born King of all Britain
   b) Arthur must be the true-born King of all Britain
   c) Arthur brought him the sword
   d) Arthur had pulled the sword from the anvil.

3. Arthur said that:
   a) he could not find Sir Kay's own sword
   b) he knew where there was another sword
   c) he found no-one guarding the sword
   d) all of the above.

4. Sir Ector told Arthur that he:
   a) was the true-born King
   b) had truly pulled out the sword
   c) should kneel before him
   d) should keep the sword as his own.

B Answer in complete sentences.

1. Why did Sir Kay say he had pulled out the sword?
2. Why do you think Sir Ector did not believe him?
3. Why do you think Arthur was puzzled by the trouble over the sword?
4. What do you think a "scabbard" is? What makes you think so?
5. What do you think will happen next?

C Answer in more than one sentence.

Explain fully how Sir Ector found out the truth.

Changing sentences

We can often say the **same** thing in **different ways**.

I am not at all happy. I am unhappy.
She cast a magic charm. She cast a spell.

A Change the underlined words in these sentences, but **keep the same meaning**.

1. He is not a bad boy.
2. She was in need of a drink.
3. I will be back in a very short time.
4. There was a considerable amount of noise.
5. The noise continued all night.
6. The sea was stormy and unpleasant.
7. Adding two and two is not difficult.

B Rewrite these sentences in a different way, but **keep the same meaning**.

1. He is very neat and tidy in the way he dresses.
2. He has great strength.
3. That camera cost a great deal of money.
4. I am very fond of chocolate.
5. She is always complaining and moaning.
6. The first letters of his name are H.L.
7. He cannot find his pen.
8. We are away from danger here.

Legends are often written in a different style from everyday English.

Arthur knew nothing of what the sword was.

In **everyday English** we would say:

Arthur did not know what the sword was.

C Change these sentences into **everyday English**.

1. He looked for the sword, but could not come to it.
2. She awaited the signal.
3. He drew forth the sword out of the anvil.
4. Down on his knees he fell.
5. Great was his joy when he saw her.
6. She was forgetful of her promise.
7. He received of the King a bag of gold.

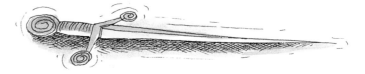

Writing for a younger audience

Write a version for younger children of the legend of Arthur and the sword in the anvil.

● Plan your story in four paragraphs.

● Write the story using words younger children will understand.

● Read your story carefully. Is everything in the right order? Have you missed anything out? Will young readers understand and enjoy it? Make any necessary changes.

● Edit your story for spelling and punctuation.

● Write a final draft.

Day 5

Homophones

Homophones are words with the **same sound**, but **different spellings**.

knight – night   rode – road   hair – hare

steel – steal   red – read

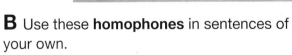

A Copy and complete each sentence with one of the **homophones** from the wordbank above.
  1. Sir Ector is a _____ .
  2. Owls fly at _____ .
  3. I have just _____ a good book.
  4. _____ is my favourite colour.
  5. He drove the car down the _____ .
  6. Arthur _____ his horse to the church.
  7. It is wrong to _____ .
  8. The sword was made of _____ .
  9. A _____ is like a large rabbit.
  10. A bald man has no _____ on his head.

B Use these **homophones** in sentences of your own.
  1. allowed   2. aloud   3. ate   4. eight
  5. great   6. grate   7. hear   8. here
  9. reign   10. rain

C Do the same with these **homophones**. Use them in sentences of your own.
  1. knew   2. new   3. knot   4. not
  5. missed   6. mist   7. meat   8. meet
  9. throne   10. thrown

The Adventures of Rama and Sita

A favourite Hindu story tells how one of the most important gods, Vishnu, came to Earth and lived as Prince Rama.

A demon called Ravana kidnaps Rama's wife, Sita. With the help of his brother, Lakshman, and the monkey warrior Hanuman, Rama raises an army to rescue her.

At the end of the first day's fighting, Lakshman was badly wounded. But Hanuman was at hand to apply healing herbs to the Prince's wounds, and Lakshman was soon able to take part in the battle again.

For many days and nights the fighting continued, and at first it seemed as if Ravana and his demons would triumph; but gradually the tide of fortune began to turn in favour of Rama. One by one, Ravana's most powerful warriors fell before the magic arrows of Rama. In desperation the Demon King decided to force his giant brother to enter the fray.

Now this giant brother was the strongest of all the demons, an enormous monster of a fellow!

Unfortunately he had always been a great source of trouble to Ravana. When he moved, his huge clumsy limbs were apt to cause much damage to buildings and gardens, and his appetite was so great that it could never be satisfied. As a result, Ravana had forced the poor giant to pass his days in slumber, and only twice a year was he allowed to wake up and enjoy a few hours' freedom.

It was not the proper season for the demon giant to be awakened, but Ravana gave orders that he should be roused instantly and told of the desperate plight of the demon armies.

The awakening of the giant was something of a problem, for though the demons clapped their hands and shouted, he did not move; nor did his peaceful snoring cease when trumpets were sounded in his ears. Elephants and camels were then brought into the giant's massive apartment, and made to trumpet and bellow, but still he slept. It was not until the animals were driven over his great body that he stirred and asked in a drowsy voice, "Why am I disturbed before the appointed time?"

The demons hastily explained why they had been forced to rouse him, and the giant muttered: "Ravana has been foolish to anger Rama and these monkeys. But to please my brother I will march against them."

So after he had refreshed himself with great quantities of food and wine, the demon giant stumbled out to battle.

The appearance of this terrible giant caused quite a panic amongst the monkeys, thousands of whom were killed as he went crashing through their ranks.

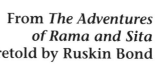

From *The Adventures of Rama and Sita* retold by Ruskin Bond

Day 1

The battle

Read the passage, then answer each question.

A Choose the answer which tells what the legend really says.
1. The Demon King was:
   a) Ravana   **b)** Rama   **c)** Lakshman   **d)** a giant.
2. Ravana's giant brother:
   a) had an enormous appetite
   b) clumsily destroyed buildings **c)** slept most of the time
   d) all of the above.
3. It was difficult to wake the giant because:
   a) of the desperate plight of the demon armies
   b) he slept so soundly no noise would wake him
   c) he had just gone to sleep   **d)** none of the above.
4. When the giant appeared, Rama's monkeys:
   a) stumbled out of the battle   **b)** marched against him
   c) began to panic   **d)** killed thousands of the enemy.

B Answer in complete sentences.
1. Who is the most important character in this extract? What makes you think so?
2. Explain why Ravana's brother was a problem to him.
3. How was the giant woken up?
4. Why do you think he stumbled out to battle?
5. What effect did the giant have when he entered the battle?

C Answer in more than one sentence.

Is this story a myth, a legend or a fable? What makes you think so?

Day 2

Nouns

Nouns are **naming** words for people, places or things.

Most nouns are **common nouns**:
elephant, ear, day, building, pen, bag, girl, camel

Proper nouns are the special names of people, places or animals. Proper nouns always begin with a capital letter:
Rama, India, Cardiff, Vicky, Rover

Collective nouns name a group of people or things:
army, crowd, flock, herd.

A Find ten **common nouns** in the extract from *The Adventures of Rama and Sita*. Make a list.

B Use each noun in your list in a sentence of your own.

C Find three **proper nouns** in the extract. Use each one in a sentence of your own.

D Copy and complete these phrases with a suitable **collective noun**. Use each phrase in a sentence of your own.
1. an _____ of soldiers
2. a _____ of sheep
3. a _____ of bees
4. a _____ of sailors
5. a _____ of ships
6. a _____ of people
7. a _____ of cards
8. a _____ of players

Making notes for retelling a story

Read again the extract from *The Adventures of Rama and Sita*. Make notes of the story outline, as preparation for telling the story to others in the class.

Use these three headings to help you structure your notes.
● Beginning
● Middle
● End

Notes for the first paragraph have been done for you.

Beginning End of 1st day Lakshman badly wounded. Hanuman applied healing herbs, L. able to fight again.

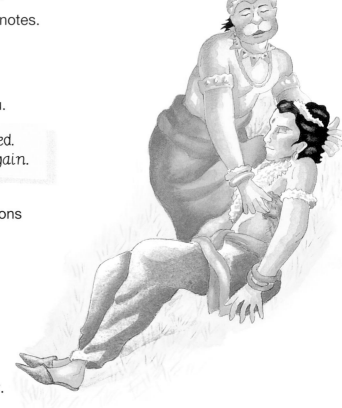

Write only the most important words. Use abbreviations where suitable.

Preparing for your story telling

Read your notes carefully. Are they clear? Have you missed anything out?

Practise using your notes to retell the story.

Use your notes to write your own version of the story.

What does it really mean?

The meaning of this sentence is not clear.

Dan asked his brother to look for his pen.

The sentence might have two different meanings:

Dan had lost his pen and asked his brother to look for it.

or

His brother had lost his pen and Dan asked him to look for it.

A Write the two possible meanings of each of these sentences.
1. Sangita told Jan her tea was ready.
2. The teacher asked Carly to take her book to the staffroom.
3. Joseph waited for Sam outside his house.

B Do the same with these. Write the two possible meanings of each sentence.
1. When Katy met Sophie she was crossing the bridge.
2. Nick waited with his brother until his bus came.
3. Amy got on well with Elena because she appreciated her jokes.
4. Pete handed Lee his bat.
5. When Ellie saw Ann she was hurrying to school.

C Write the four possible meanings of this sentence. Ask yourself these questions: Who had lost the ball? Who did the ball belong to?

Jake was impatient with Gary because he had lost his ball.

Fantastical Beasts

These are some of the many fantastical beasts from myths and legends.

The Manticore

The manticore is a man-eating fabulous beast from Persia. It has the head of a man, the body of a lion, a porcupine's quills and the tail of a scorpion. It has three rows of teeth and the sting on its tail can be shot like an arrow. The manticore was first mentioned in the fifth century BC in a Greek history of Persia.

The Griffin

The griffin is the offspring of a lion and an eagle. Its legs and all from its shoulders to its head are like an eagle. The rest of its body is that of a lion. The griffin keeps guard over hidden treasures.

A Dragon

A dragon is a large winged crocodile with a serpent's tail. Its name comes from the Greek word *drakon*, meaning "to see" or "to look at". In stories, dragons often watch over treasure or captive ladies.

The Sirens

These are half woman and half bird. They sing songs so sweet that sailors who hear them forget everything but their song and die of hunger. A Greek hero, Ulysses, defeated the charm of their song by filling his companions' ears with wax and tying himself to the mast of his ship.

The Gorgons

The gorgons are hideous women with serpents instead of hair. They have claws and monstrous teeth, and one glance turns their victims to stone.

Cerberus

Cerberus is the three-headed dog that guards the entrance to the underworld in Greek mythology.

The Minotaur

The Minotaur is the monster that lived in a maze or labyrinth on the island of Crete. It had the head and horns of a bull and the body of a man. Its food was human flesh. Every spring seven maidens and seven youths were sent from Greece as tribute to King Minos. They were put into the labyrinth, which was so cleverly constructed that no one could find their way out again. One by one the Minotaur ate them all.

Beasts from myths and legends

Read the descriptions of the beasts on page 43.

A Match each beast to its description. Do it like this:

Cerberus: three-headed dog

Beast	Description
Cerberus	half woman, half bird
Gorgons	large winged crocodile with a serpent's tail
Sirens	hideous women with serpents instead of hair
Manticore	three-headed dog
Griffin	head and horns of a bull, body of a man
Dragon	head of a man, body of lion, porcupine's quills and tail of a scorpion
Minotaur	head and shoulders of an eagle, body of a lion

S

Day 2

Personal pronouns

A **pronoun** is a word that is used **in place of a noun**.

Personal pronouns are used for **people** and **things**.

> I   me   you   he   she   it
> we   us   you   they   them

A Copy and complete with a suitable **personal pronoun**.
1. Where are _____ going?
2. _____ are walking to school.
3. _____ will come with _____ to the shops.
4. _____ came first in the race, but _____ was second.
5. _____ are going swimming. Would _____ like to come with _____?
6. The Bennings have a dog. _____ are taking _____ for a walk.
7. _____ have left my books at school. Will _____ get _____ for _____?

B Use each of the **personal pronouns** above in a sentence of your own.

B Answer in complete sentences.
1. Which beasts act as guards?
2. Which beasts are part bird?
3. Which is the only beast with the body of a man?
4. In what ways are the Sirens and Gorgons alike?
5. In what ways are they different?
6. Explain the reason for the name "dragon".

C Answer in more than one sentence.

Why do you think the author chose the title "Fantastical Beasts?"

C Rewrite these sentences by using a suitable **personal pronoun**. The first one has been done for you.
1. Dad and Joe went fishing, but <u>Dad and Joe</u> didn't catch anything.
   Dad and Joe went fishing, but they didn't catch anything.
2. Taz and I love reading and <u>Taz and I</u> are going to the library.
3. Patrick and Liam woke up a big dog which chased <u>Patrick and Liam</u>.
4. Tina and I found an interesting book. <u>Tina and I</u> read <u>the book</u> together.
5. When Anita and Tom entered the competition, <u>Anita</u> won first prize and <u>Tom</u> won the second. <u>Anita and Tom</u> were very pleased.

Days 3 and 4

Making notes

Choose four of the fantastical beasts described on page 43. Make notes about each one.
Use your notes to write a description of each beast in your own words.

Making notes

● Write only the most important words.

● Use abbreviations where suitable: 3 for 'three', ½ for 'half', initials for the second time you write the same name, e.g. P for Persia.

Checking your notes

● Are your notes clear? Have you missed anything out?

Using your notes

● Think about your audience, and how you will present the information.

● Use your notes to write about each beast in your own words. This is easier if you do not look back at the original text.

● Keep your audience in mind as you write. Choose your words carefully to suit your reader.

● Illustrate your writing with your own pictures of the fantastical beasts.

Use information books or IT sources to find out about one of these fantastical beasts:

● the phoenix   ● the unicorn   ● the hippogriff   ● the yeti   ● the Loch Ness monster

Make notes and write about the beast in your own words.

Day 5

Who, whose and which

Who and **which** are **relative pronouns**.
They link people or things already mentioned.
Who and **whose** refer to people.
Which refers to things.

A Copy and complete these sentences with **who**, **whose** or **which**.
1. The boy _____ won the race is called Simon.
2. That is the book _____ I left on the bus.
3. This is the man _____ rescued my daughter.
4. The letter _____ I sent last week has only just arrived.
5. The lady _____ keys we found gave us a reward.
6. The pen _____ you lent me is similar to my father's.
7. The man _____ kitten you found is very pleased.
8. He bought a watch _____ was very expensive.

The young men and maidens who were sent to Crete were eaten by the Minotaur. Ariadne, **whose** father was King Minos, decided to help Theseus.
She drew a sword **which** she gave him.

B Join these sentences using **who** or **which**. The first one has been done for you.
1. The man found her purse. The man was a friend of mine.
   The man who found her purse was a friend of mine.
2. The girl won the prize. She is my sister.
3. This is John. He built our garage.
4. This is our garage. John built it.
5. I went home in my uncle's car. He has just bought it.
6. The boy lives next door to me. He knows your aunty.
7. He hid the money in a box. He then buried it.

45

Theseus and the Minotaur

Ariadne has given Theseus a magic sword and a ball of wool to help him fight the Minotaur.

"Once you have slain the Minotaur, you must find your way out of the maze. When you get in, tie one end of the wool to the doorpost and let the ball unroll as you go. You have only to follow the wool back and you will find your way out."

Theseus listened carefully to these instructions, and early in the morning the young men and maidens were led to the entrance of the maze. Their guards opened the great bronze door and drove them in. As soon as the door was locked behind them, Theseus bade his companions remain hidden close to the beginning of the maze. They wished him good fortune as he fastened the end of the woollen ball to the doorpost and made his way forward, gripping firmly in his right hand the sword which Ariadne had given him. Through the cunning labyrinth he stole, this way and that, listening intently for any sound the hidden monster might make. As he went, the ball of wool gradually unwound, until very little of it was left in the pocket of his tunic. Suddenly he heard the sound of snorting and the scuffling of some clumsy body. He judged that the Minotaur must be round the next corner of the passage he was exploring. Almost before he knew it, the creature was in front of him, scarcely a stone's throw away. He saw the great black head, the cruel horns, the wicked eyes, and even Theseus's heart began to thump. Nevertheless, he tightened his grip on the sword and awaited the charge that must surely come. Sure enough, the Minotaur lowered its head, gave a terrifying bellow and rushed towards Theseus. Nimbly the young man jumped to one side, and as the

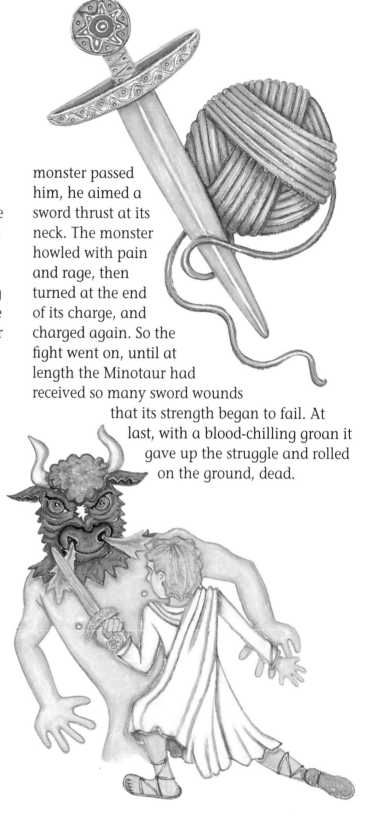

monster passed him, he aimed a sword thrust at its neck. The monster howled with pain and rage, then turned at the end of its charge, and charged again. So the fight went on, until at length the Minotaur had received so many sword wounds that its strength began to fail. At last, with a blood-chilling groan it gave up the struggle and rolled on the ground, dead.

From *Giants and Warriors* retold by James Reeves

Day 1 — Ariadne's gifts

Read the passage, then answer each question.

A Choose the answer which tells what the story really says.
1. Theseus was told to:
   a) tie one end of the wool to the doorpost
   b) listen for the snorting and scuffling of the monster
   c) lead the young men and maidens into the maze
   d) all of the above.
2. The Minotaur:
   a) was waiting just inside the door
   b) had a great black head   c) was killed with a stone
   d) none of the above.
3. The "cunning labyrinth" was:
   a) a monster with the head of a bull
   b) an enchanted sword   c) a ball of wool
   d) a maze of passages.
4. The monster died because:
   a) Theseus struck it with a single mighty blow
   b) it received so many sword wounds its strength began to fail
   c) it rolled on the ground
   d) it gave a blood-chilling groan.

B Answer in complete sentences.
1. Why do you think Theseus told his companions to hide close to the beginning of the maze?
2. Explain why he listened intently as he moved through the maze.
3. Was Theseus afraid at any time? How can you tell?
4. Explain how the monster attempted to kill Theseus.
5. What do you think will happen next? What makes you think so?

C Answer in more than one sentence.

If you were Theseus what would you have done if the ball of wool had run out before you found the Minotaur? Give a reason for your answer.

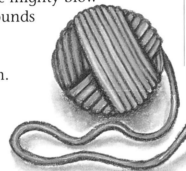

Day 2 — Its and it's

Its shows that something belongs to a thing or an animal.

> The Minotaur lowered its head.

It's is short for **it is.**

> It's an enchanted sword.

A Copy and complete these sentences with **its** or **it's.**
1. The cat ate ___ dinner.
2. ___ time for sport.
3. The dog has lost ___ bone.
4. The budgie flew back into ___ cage.
5. I think ___ cruel to keep animals in cages.
6. This book has lost ___ cover.

B Write two sentences of your own using the words **its**, and two sentences using **it's.**

Possessive pronouns

Possessive pronouns show who or what owns them:
mine ours yours his hers theirs

> This is your sword. This sword is **yours.**

> This is her cloak. This cloak is **hers.**

Ours, hers, yours and **theirs** never have apostrophes.

C Copy and complete these sentences with a **possessive pronoun.**
1. This is our house. This house is ___.
2. That is your scarf. That scarf is ___.
3. He looked after his bag, but she has lost ___.
4. You bring your sandwiches and I will bring ___.
5. These are their shoes. These shoes are ___.
6. This bat belongs to James. This bat is ___.

D Use these **possessive pronouns** in sentences of your own.
1. hers   2. theirs   3. mine
4. yours   5. ours   6. his

Days 3 and 4

Killing a monster

Write a story, in traditional style, about a hero or heroine who fights and kills a fantastical beast.

Characters

- Invent a hero or heroine.
- Choose one of the creatures described on page 43, or invent one of your own.

Setting

- Choose a lonely place for the setting.

Plot

- What weapon or other aid does the main character have? How does he or she get these things?
- How does he or she meet the monster?
- What happens then?
- How does the story end?

Day 5

Adjectival clauses

When a phrase contains a verb it is called a clause.

An **adjectival clause** tells us **more** about a **noun**.

> Ariadne, **who was the daughter of King Minos**, gave Theseus an enchanted sword.

> Theseus, **who was a brave young man**, killed the Minotaur.

- Adjectival clauses begin with these words: **who**, **whose**, **which**.
- Notice that commas are used to separate an adjectival clause from the rest of the sentence.

A Copy each sentence and underline the **adjectival clause**.

1. King Midas, who was a stern man, would not listen to his daughter.
2. The Minotaur, which had the head of a bull and the body of a man, lived in a labyrinth.
3. Mr Jones, who is a friend of my father, cycles twenty miles a day.
4. Phil, who is six feet tall, is the only boy who can see over the fence.
5. Our car, which is an old one, broke down in the high street.
6. Yasmin, whose hair is long, has decided to have it cut very short.

B Copy and complete each sentence with an **adjectival clause** of your own.

1. Jenny, who _____, is my best friend.
2. This book, which _____, is a very good read.
3. Paul, who _____, has been selected for the football team.
4. This ring, which _____, cost a lot of money.
5. Lee, who _____, is now back at school.
6. Carla, who _____, is the fastest runner in the school.

C Write six sentences of your own with adjectival clauses.

48

Myths

Myths often explain how things came to be.

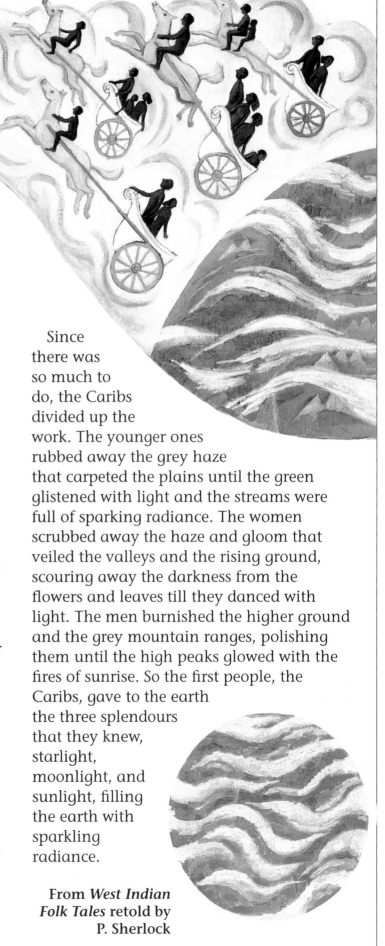

The Caribs were the first people. There were no other people before them. Their first home was the moon. They knew light and dark, day and night, and they obeyed the Ancient One, Kabo Tano.

In the bright procession of worlds that moved around them the Caribs saw one that never gleamed with light, but remained veiled by a thick, grey haze that grew duller and greyer with each passing season. If at times the veil lifted for a brief period there stood revealed bleak mountain peaks rising out of inky darkness.

The oldest Carib pointed to the dark, spinning earth and said to his youngest grandchild, "It's a dull earth. It needs cleaning."

A young Carib girl, combing her long black hair, pointed to the earth and said, "It seems to get duller and duller. What that earth needs is a good polishing."

The strongest of the young men among the Caribs of the Moon asked his companions, "How can we put up year after year with this dull earth? Other generations have done nothing about it. Let us show what we can do. Our strength can transform the dull earth into a silver world like our Moon."

So the Caribs descended to earth on their cloud chariots. As they drew near they marvelled at the bleakness of the towering peaks and at the thickness of the haze resting like a grey carpet on the plains and pastureland. "We have much work to do," said the oldest Carib. "This haze has been getting thicker and darker year after year."

Since there was so much to do, the Caribs divided up the work. The younger ones rubbed away the grey haze that carpeted the plains until the green glistened with light and the streams were full of sparking radiance. The women scrubbed away the haze and gloom that veiled the valleys and the rising ground, scouring away the darkness from the flowers and leaves till they danced with light. The men burnished the higher ground and the grey mountain ranges, polishing them until the high peaks glowed with the fires of sunrise. So the first people, the Caribs, gave to the earth the three splendours that they knew, starlight, moonlight, and sunlight, filling the earth with sparkling radiance.

From *West Indian Folk Tales* retold by P. Sherlock

The Caribs

Read the passage, then answer each question.

A Choose the answer which tells what the myth really says.
1. The first home of the Caribs was:
   a) the sun   **b)** the moon   **c)** the earth
   d) bleak mountain peaks.
2. The Caribs saw that the dullness of the earth was:
   a) growing duller and greyer
   b) due to bleak mountain peaks
   c) getting slowly brighter
   d) none of the above.
3. The strongest young man suggested that they:
   a) clean the earth   **b)** polish the earth
   c) make it a silver world like the moon
   d) obey the Ancient One, Kabo Tano.
4. The Carib women: **a)** burnished the higher ground
   b) made the streams full of sparking radiance
   c) polished the mountains
   d) scrubbed away the haze and gloom.
5. The Caribs gave to the earth:
   a) starlight, moonlight and sunlight
   b) starlight, moonlight, and bright flowers
   c) moonlight, sunlight and streams
   d) starlight, sunlight and silver clouds.

B Answer in complete sentences.
1. What does this story explain?
2. What do you think "the bright procession of worlds" is?
3. How, and why, did the Caribs descend to earth?
4. Who do you think Kabo Tano was? Give a reason for your answer.
5. Do you think the Caribs stayed on earth after they cleaned it? What makes you think so?

C Answer in more than one sentence.

Did you enjoy reading this story? Explain the reasons for your answer.

Antonyms

An **antonym** is a word with an **opposite** meaning to another:

dull – bright thick – thin   dark – light

A Write an **antonym** for each of these words.
1. strong   2. first   3. day   4. out
5. oldest   6. clean   7. good   8. near

B Some words have more than one antonym. Write as many **antonyms** as you can for each of these words.
1. big   2. dull   3. right   4. young
5. sad   6. cold   7. stop   8. dirty

C Choose one **antonym** for each of the words in **B**. Use each one in a sentence of your own.

D Some words make their opposites by adding a **prefix**:
tie – **un**tie   agree – **dis**agree

Make **antonyms** from the words below by adding one of these prefixes.

un-   dis-   im-   in-   non-   mis-

1. comfortable   2. active   3. possible
4. sense   5. sufficient   6. behave   7. fiction
8. believe   9. patient   10. capable

E Choose six of the **antonyms** you have made in **D**. Use each one in a sentence.

Days 3 and 4

Writing your own myth

Write your own myth explaining how the first people came to live on Earth, and how they changed it.

● Who might those first people have been? How, and why, did they come here?

● What did they find? How did they change things?

Planning

● Decide who you are writing the story for.

● Decide how you will present your story.

● Plan your story in three or four paragraphs.

Writing and reviewing

● Write a first draft, keeping your audience in mind.

● Review your first draft.

● Write an improved second draft.

● Edit your second draft.

Presenting

● Write a final corrected draft of your story, ready for your audience.

S

Day 5

Constructing sentences

A Change the **word order** in these sentences so that the **meaning stays the same**.
1. Lightning burned houses and knocked down trees.
2. He helped with the housework in the morning.
3. After tea they went for a long walk.
4. The Caribs brought starlight, moonlight and sunlight.
5. He gave me the box with a smile on his face.

B Make these sentences as **short** as you can by deleting all the less important words. Keep the **meaning the same**. The first one has been done for you.
1. The man with a long beard lifted the heavy box.
   The man lifted the box.
2. After school Jack went home as quickly as he could.
3. The old woman in the red coat got on a number 58 bus to Upton Downs.
4. As the sun was setting she took her eager dog for a walk in the park.
5. Not looking where he was going, and running at top speed, Tom crashed into a passing man.
6. He watched the old, rusty tugboat through a pair of brand new binoculars.
7. Sitting very quietly in a comfortable chair, he read the book from cover to cover.

C Add words to these sentences to make them **more interesting**.
1. The dog chased the man.
2. I like fruit.
3. She climbed the hill.
4. She drove a car.
5. The boy watched the man.
6. He opened the door.
7. The girl packed the suitcase.
8. The man ate a meal.

Rain, Thunder and Lightning

The Water Cycle

Water can never be used up or run out completely. The rain that falls from the clouds will eventually return to the sky to fall again.

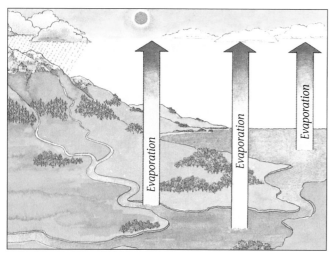

A large sewerage works in Essex

The water in the sea, rivers and lakes is evaporated by the sun and rises into the sky as invisible water vapour. At the same time, water evaporates from plants and trees on the land.

When this water vapour rises higher and higher to where the air is much colder, it cools down. The cooling causes it to condense into droplets of water which become visible again. Clouds are made up of billions of such water droplets. The clouds are carried from place to place by air currents. If the clouds become cold enough then the droplets get bigger and fall as rain. If it is colder still the droplets freeze and fall as snow or hail.

Rain seeps into the ground until it meets non-porous rock which stops it from sinking any further. Rivers collect this water and carry it to lakes and the sea. The water is evaporated by the sun and the water cycle begins all over again.

The water we use at home is stored in reservoirs. When it is needed it is piped to a water treatment plant where it passes through filters to remove dirt and harmful bacteria. The purified water is then piped to homes.

Waste water from homes goes into the sewerage system and on to a water treatment works. The solid waste is removed, and then the water goes through a different process to remove bacteria and other harmful substances. Oxygen is then added to the water so that different, useful bacteria can clean the water further. Only after this final cleaning process is it passed into rivers and eventually into the sea.

The water cycle

Read the passage, then answer each question.

A Choose the answer which tells what the passage really says.

1. The water in the sea:
   a) rises into the sky as water vapour
   b) has fallen as rain
   c) seeps into the ground
   d) is purified and piped to our homes.

2. Condensation means:
   a) steamy windows
   b) removing bacteria and other harmful substances
   c) water changing into water vapour
   d) water vapour changing back into droplets of water.

3. Evaporation is caused by:
   a) the sun   b) clouds   c) reservoirs
   d) water treatment works.

4. Snow is tiny water droplets that have:
   a) condensed   b) evaporated
   c) frozen   d) become hailstones.

5. Oxygen is added at the water treatment works:
   a) to help with evaporation   b) to keep fish healthy
   c) so that bacteria can clean the water further
   d) to remove harmful substances.

B Answer in complete sentences.

1. Explain how water rises from the sea to become clouds.
2. Explain how hail is formed.
3. What do you think "non-porous" means? What makes you think so?
4. What is removed from water before it is piped to our homes? Why?
5. Why do you think waste water is treated *after* it leaves our homes?

C Answer in more than one sentence.

Explain why water can never be used up or run out completely.

S

Saying the same thing in a different way

A Change the word order in each sentence so that the **meaning is the same**.

1. It rained all day last Sunday.
2. Yesterday I bought a new umbrella.
3. My favourite sport is rugby.
4. Reeta is my best friend.
5. Along the road she walked.
6. He climbed over the wall.
7. Like a mirror shone the lake.
8. The roof collapsed without warning.

B Do the same with these. **Change the word order** in each sentence so that the **meaning is the same**.

1. Inside the room there was an enormous sofa.
2. There was a loud cheer when Nick came on the field.
3. Before water is piped to our homes it is purified.
4. After waste water leaves our homes it goes to a water treatment plant.
5. Until that moment he did not realise how popular he was.
6. He read her letter during the break.

C Write each sentence in a different way so that the **meaning is the same**. Change any words necessary.

1. It is raining cats and dogs.
2. He wanted to say something but held his tongue.
3. I was very angry with Tom.
4. I found the work exhausting.
5. The water in the sea is evaporated by the sun.
6. Clouds are carried from place to place by air currents.
7. He took a deep breath and dived into the water.

Explaining things

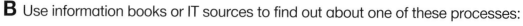

A Read about water purification on page 52. Make careful notes. Use your notes to write an explanation of the process in your own words.

B Use information books or IT sources to find out about one of these processes:

● the life cycle of a butterfly

● the life cycle of a frog

● how to find a percentage

● how a letter is collected, sorted and delivered

● how a household appliance works, e.g. a fridge

● how glass is made

● how a TV picture is sent to your home.

Make notes on the process and write down the titles, authors and publishers of the books or IT sources you use.

Explain the process in your own words. Use diagrams to make your explanation clear.

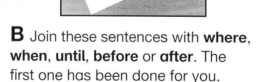

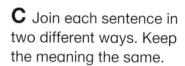

Joining sentences

A Join these sentences with **who**, **whose** or **which**. The first one has been done for you.

1. I met a man. The man knew my uncle.
   I met a man who knew my uncle.
2. This is the water treatment plant. It purifies our water.
3. That is Bill Johnson. He is going to live in Canada.
4. This is a picture of a lake. The lake is very deep.
5. I bought a radio. It would not work.
6. I met a girl. Her mother is our dinner lady.
7. These are the Smiths. Their children go to our school.

B Join these sentences with **where**, **when**, **until**, **before** or **after**. The first one has been done for you.

1. I'll meet you there. We met there last week.
   I'll meet you where we met last week.
2. They sat there. It was quiet in that place.
3. It gets cold. The sun goes down.
4. We can't leave. Mum comes back.
5. He ate his tea. He worked on the car.
6. She painted the door. She went out.
7. He read the book. It was time for school.

C Join each sentence in two different ways. Keep the meaning the same.

1. I borrowed a lawn mower. It would not work.
2. He repaired the car. He went on holiday.
3. This is a beautiful photograph. It is a photograph of the Alps.
4. He injured his leg. He could not walk.

Bishop Hatto

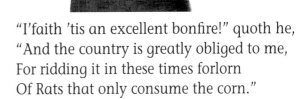

*Robert Southey's poem tells us the story of how
Bishop Hatto was punished for a terrible crime.*

The summer and autumn had been so wet,
That in winter the corn was growing yet,
'Twas a piteous sight to see all around
The grain lie rotting on the ground.

Every day the starving poor,
Crowded around Bishop Hatto's door,
For he had a plentiful last year's store,
And all the neighbourhood could tell
His granaries were furnish'd well.

At last Bishop Hatto appointed a day
To quiet the poor without delay;
He bade them to his great Barn repair,
And they should have food for the winter there.

Rejoiced such tidings good to hear,
The poor folk flock'd from far and near;
The great Barn was full as it could hold
Of women and children, and young and old.

Then when he saw it could hold no more,
Bishop Hatto he made fast the door;
And while for mercy on Christ they call,
He set fire to the Barn and burnt them all.

"I'faith 'tis an excellent bonfire!" quoth he,
"And the country is greatly obliged to me,
For ridding it in these times forlorn
Of Rats that only consume the corn."

So then to his palace returned he,
And he sat down to supper merrily,
And he slept that night like an innocent man;
But Bishop Hatto never slept again.

In the morning as he enter'd the hall
Where his picture hung against the wall,
A sweat like death all over him came,
For the Rats had eaten it out of the frame.

As he look'd there came a man from his farm,
He had a countenance white with alarm;
"My Lord, I open'd your granaries this morn,
And the Rats had eaten all your corn."

Another came running presently,
And he was pale as pale could be.
"Fly! my Lord Bishop, fly," quoth he,
"Ten thousand Rats are coming this way, ...
The Lord forgive you for yesterday!"

"I'll go to my tower on the Rhine," replied he,
"'Tis the safest place in Germany;
The walls are high and the shores are steep,
And the stream is strong and the water deep."

Bishop Hatto fearfully hasten'd away,
And he crost the Rhine without delay,
And reach'd his tower, and barr'd with care
All the windows, doors, and loop-holes there.

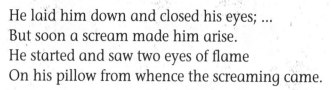

He laid him down and closed his eyes; ...
But soon a scream made him arise.
He started and saw two eyes of flame
On his pillow from whence the screaming came.

He listen'd and look'd; ... it was only the Cat;
But the Bishop he grew more fearful for that,
For she sat screaming, mad with fear,
At the Army of Rats that were drawing near.

For they have swum over the river so deep,
And they have climb'd the shores so steep,
And up to the Tower their way is bent,
To do the work for which they were sent.

They are not to be told by the dozen or score,
By thousands they come, and by myriads and more,
Such numbers have never been heard of before,
Such a judgement had never been witness'd of yore.

Down on his knees the Bishop fell,
And faster and faster his beads did he tell,
As louder and louder drawing near
The gnawing of their teeth he could hear.

And in at the windows and in at the door,
And through the walls helter-skelter they pour,
And down from the ceiling and up through the floor,
From the right and the left, from behind and before,
From within and without, from above and below,
And all at once to the Bishop they go.

They have whetted their teeth against the stones,
And now they pick the Bishop's bones;
They gnaw'd the flesh from every limb,
For they were sent to do judgement on him!

Robert Southey

Day 1

A terrible crime

Read the poem, then answer each question.

A Choose the answer which tells what the poem really says.
1. The poor were starving because:
   a) they had no money   **b)** the grain was rotting
   c) Bishop Hatto had bought all the grain that year
   d) the shops were closed.
2. They went to the bishop because:
   a) his barn was big enough to hold them all
   b) he was a generous man
   c) he had grain from the previous year
   d) they were afraid of the approaching rats.
3. The corn in the bishop's granaries was eaten by: **a)** rats
   b) the poor   **c)** the bishop and his friends
   d) the family of a man from his farm.
4. The bishop thought he was safe from the rats because:
   a) his tower was the safest in Germany
   b) its walls were high
   c) the river was deep and its shores steep
   d) all of the above.
5. The rats came to the tower because:
   a) they were sent to do judgement on the bishop
   b) they were hungry   **c)** they were looking for grain
   d) all of the above.

B Answer in complete sentences.
1. Why do you think Bishop Hatto burned the barn?
2. How did he justify his action?
3. Why was it appropriate that rats caused his death?
4. Explain why the bishop thought he would be safe from the rats in his tower.
5. Pick out one or two lines from the poem which you think are particularly effective. Say why you think so.

C Answer in more than one sentence.

How does the poem make you feel? Which words and phrases make you feel that way?

Day 2

Letter strings with different sounds

Read these words and listen to the sounds: g**oo**d f**oo**d p**oo**r

Each word has the same letter string **oo**, but a different sound.

A Find the **rhyming pairs**.

rein   treat   late   taste   off
main   meat   waist   now
cough   bough   great

B Find a word to **rhyme** with each of these words. The first one has been done for you.
1. hear *deer*   2. through
3. bread   4. though
5. great   6. bought
7. soup   8. hall
9. pour   10. shall

C Find as many words as you can with the same letter string but a **different sound**. The first one has been done for you.
1. b*ough* – *bought, cough, rough, though, through*
2. head   3. fork   4. rein   5. field

D Choose five of the words you found in **C** and use each one in a sentence of your own.

Find as many words as you can which rhyme with these words.
   1. rough   2. bough   3. through   4. rule
   5. rein   6. store   7. could   8. climb

Writing verse

A Use one of these ideas for a new verse for the poem "**Bishop Hatto**".

● the cat leaves the tower in fear

● people flee from the advancing rats

● a servant finds the bishop's bones.

B Choose one or two verses from the poem. Rewrite them with new ideas and words of your own.

Note that each verse of "**Bishop Hatto**" has four lines, and an **AABB** rhyming pattern.

Day 5

Antonyms

An antonym is a word with an opposite meaning to another.

A Find words in the poem **"Bishop Hatto"** which are **antonyms** of these words.
1. shallow
2. weak
3. ever
4. play
5. low
6. empty
7. small
8. none

B Add **prefixes** to these words to make **antonyms**. Use each one in a sentence.
1. tie
2. safe
3. correct
4. like
5. certain
6. visible
7. understand
8. expensive

C Find **a single word** with the same meaning as these phrases. Then write an **antonym**. The first one has been done for you.
1. cannot be done – *impossible, possible*
2. pleased as punch
3. down in the dumps
4. lend a hand
5. roar with laughter
6. having no doubts
7. after dark

D Write an **antonym and a phrase** with an opposite meaning to each of these words. The first one has been done for you.
1. wet – *dry, as dry as a bone*
2. noisy
3. soft
4. dull
5. bent
6. slow
7. tiny
8. heavy
9. timid

E Use each of your phrases from **D** in a sentence of your own.

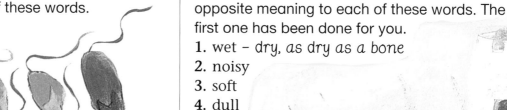

58

Cautionary Tales

Matilda
Who told Lies, and was Burned to Death

Matilda told such dreadful lies,
It made one gasp and stretch one's eyes;
Her Aunt, who, from her earliest youth,
Had kept a strict regard for truth,
Attempted to believe Matilda:
The effort very nearly killed her,
And would have done so, had not she
Discovered this infirmity.
For once, towards the close of day,
Matilda, growing tired of play,
And finding she was left alone,
Went tiptoe to the telephone
And summoned the immediate aid
Of London's noble fire-brigade.
Within an hour the gallant band
Were pouring in on every hand,
From Putney, Hackney Downs, and Bow
With courage high and hearts a-glow
They galloped, roaring through the town,
"Matilda's house is burning down!"
Inspired by British cheers and loud
Proceeding from the frenzied crowd,
They ran their ladders through a score
Of windows on the ballroom floor;
And took peculiar pains to souse
The pictures up and down the house,
Until Matilda's Aunt succeeded
In showing them they were not needed;
And even then she had to pay
To get the men to go away!

It happened that a few weeks later
Her Aunt was off to the theatre
To see that interesting play
The Second Mrs. Tanqueray,
She had refused to take her niece
To hear this entertaining piece:
A deprivation just and wise
To punish her for telling lies.

That night a fire *did* break out –
You should have heard Matilda shout!
You should have heard her scream and bawl,
And throw the window up and call
To people passing in the street –

(The rapidly increasing heat
Encouraging her to obtain
Their confidence) – but all in vain!
For every time she shouted "Fire!"
They only answered "Little liar!"
And therefore when her Aunt returned,
Matilda, and the house, were burned.

Hilaire Belloc

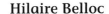

Matilda

Read the poem, then answer each question.

A Choose the answer which tells what the poem really says.

1. Matilda phoned the fire-brigade because:
   a) she was tired of playing
   b) the house was on fire
   c) she heard people shouting "Matilda's house is burning down!"
   d) none of the above.

2. The fire fighters:
   a) put the fire out   b) shouted "Little liar!"
   c) arrived within an hour   d) all of the above.

3. Her aunt left Matilda alone because:
   a) Matilda could not be trusted
   b) she wanted to punish Matilda
   c) she went to see a play
   d) she thought a fire might break out.

4. The people in the street did not believe Matilda because
   a) there was no smoke
   b) the fire fighters had only just gone
   c) she had cried fire before
   d) she had not phoned the fire-brigade.

B Answer in complete sentences.

1. What do you think is the moral of this story?
2. Why do you think her aunt at first believed Matilda's lies?
3. How might things have been different if her aunt had stayed at home?
4. Pick out lines from the poem you think are particularly effective. Say why you think so.
5. How does the poem make you feel? Give reasons for your answer.

C Answer in more than one sentence.

Do you think Matilda's aunt was wise to punish Matilda in the way she did? Give reasons for your answer.

Suffixes

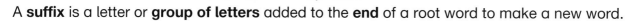

A **suffix** is a letter or **group of letters** added to the **end** of a root word to make a new word.

    courage + **ous** = courageous   entertain + **ment** = entertainment

Sometimes letters need to be changed or dropped before adding the suffix:

    prevent + **tion** = prevention   fame + **ous** = famous

A Make new words from these words by adding a suitable **suffix** from the wordbank.

-tion	-cian	-ous	-ment	-ship

1. champion   2. magic
3. invent   4. disappoint
5. poison   6. mathematics
7. partner   8. enjoy
9. correct   10. operate

B Do the same with these. Make new words from these words by adding a suitable **suffix** from the wordbank opposite.

1. decorate   2. electric
3. companion   4. relate
5. music   6. develop
7. punish   8. examine
9. nerve   10. danger

C Use the words you made in **A** in sentences of your own.

D Use five of the words you made in **B** in sentences of your own.

Read this cautionary tale, then write your own tale using the ideas on page 62.

The Boy Who Cried Wolf

Everyone was afraid of the wolf because he ate people. This gave little Harry an idea.

Whenever Harry had to do something he hated, like having a bath, he would cry, "Wolf!" (even if the wolf was nowhere to be seen). Because everybody was afraid of the wolf Harry was left alone to do just what he wanted.

Once a week Harry went for his violin lesson. Because he hated lessons he cried, "Wolf!" even though the wolf was not around. Then Harry was left alone to play the kind of music he liked. Sometimes Harry even cried, "Wolf!" just for the fun of it.

One day Harry was cycling in the mountains when the wolf jumped out of the rocks.

"WOLF!" cried Harry. He ran back to town crying, "WOLF! WOLF!" all the way.

"WOLF!" cried Harry, but his grandmother didn't believe him. Harry always cried, "Wolf!"

"Tell me another one!" she said.

"WOLF!" cried Harry, but nobody listened. "Save me from the WOLF!" shrieked Harry, but everybody laughed.

"Harry's crying 'wolf' again," they said.

At last the wolf caught up with Harry. "You shouldn't have told so many lies!" said the grown-ups sternly.

From *The Boy Who Cried Wolf* by Tony Ross

Write your own cautionary tale, either as a narrative poem or as a story. Here are some ideas you might use.

- Ahmed who never shuts doors or gates.
- Jemima who never listens.
- Harry who can never stop talking.
- Romila who never keeps things tidy.

  - Introduce your character and his or her bad habit.

  - Briefly describe an amusing incident about this habit.

  - Tell the main incident in the story.

  - Describe how it ends.

  - State the lesson to be learned from the story.

Day 5 Ambiguity

Ambiguity means having **more than one meaning**.

Ambiguity sometimes happens when sentences are shortened for headlines or signs.

> **Firemen rescue girl with ladder**

A Explain **two possible meanings** of each of these phrases.
1. Nothing tastes better than McDuff's Cookies
2. Wolf gives boy idea
3. Matilda lies
4. the best painting competition
5. a new car salesman
6. a small lady's handbag
7. Baby changing room

B Do the same with these sentences. Explain **two possible meanings** of each.
1. The boy was followed by a dog wearing jeans.
2. I saw a mother with a small baby pushing a pram.

C Rewrite each sentence in **B** so that the meaning is clear.

D Write the **four possible meanings** of this sentence.

Mum was not in a good mood when Ellie arrived because she had lost her bag.

Traditional Tales

Ali Baba was a poor woodcutter in Persia.

One day, while he was at work cutting down trees, Ali Baba saw a large cloud of dust approaching him fast. It was raised by a band of horsemen: tall, powerful men, very well mounted and armed. No robbers had ever been seen in that part of the country, but Ali Baba was afraid. He quickly climbed a tree which was overhung by a rock so steep that no one could reach the top. He felt safe here, and looking through the thick leaves he could see without being seen.

Judging by their bearing and equipment, the horsemen did indeed seem to be robbers. Ali Baba counted forty, and guessed that they plied their thieving trade far from this lonely place, but came here to meet one another.

Once the men had dismounted, each unbridled his horse, tied it up, hung a nosebag full of barley round its neck, and took off the saddle-bags, which were so heavy that Ali Baba thought they must be full of gold and silver.

The man who seemed to be captain of the band went up to the rock, passing close to the big trees where Ali Baba was hiding. He stopped, parted the bushes and brambles, and uttered the strange words: "Open, Sesame!" No sooner had he spoken them than a door in the rock opened. The robbers went in, and the door closed after them.

They stayed there in their hiding place for a long time. When the door opened again, the captain came out first, counted his men one by one, leaving no one inside, and said, "Shut, Sesame!" Then the door closed of its own accord.

Each man went back to his horse, put on its bridle again, fastened the now empty saddle-bags in place, and remounted. With the captain at their head, the horsemen set off, going back the same way as they had come.

Ali Baba watched until they had disappeared from sight. But he dared not climb down yet, fearing one of the robbers might have forgotten something and would come back for it. At last, as all was quiet, he left his post, went up to the door and spoke the words he remembered. The door opened, and he went in.

He found himself in a large, artificial cave with a very high roof. Bright light shone in through an opening in this roof, showing him the most wonderful treasures: piles of rich merchandise, silks and brocades, valuable carpets, and above all a vast quantity of gold and silver in leather bags, all piled up on top of one another.

From *The Tale of Ali Baba and the Forty Thieves* translated by Anthea Bell

Ali Baba and the Forty Thieves

Read the passage, then answer each question.

A Choose the answer which tells what the story really says.

1. As he watched from the tree Ali Baba guessed that the men came to:
   a) meet one another
   b) rob poor people like himself
   c) enter a secret cave
   d) feed their horses.

2. Ali Baba thought the saddle bags must be full of gold and silver because:
   a) he saw a flash of gold
   b) the men were thieves
   c) the bags were heavy
   d) he heard coins jingle as the men dismounted.

3. The door in the rock was hidden by:
   a) a rock so steep no one could climb it
   b) a cloud of dust
   c) the thick leaves of a tall tree
   d) bushes and brambles.

4. He stayed in his tree when the men had gone because:
   a) he was afraid they might come back
   b) they might have left someone in the cave
   c) he was thinking of what he would do with all the treasure
   d) at first the door would not open for him.

5. The cave was light inside because:
   a) wonderful lamps shone all around
   b) there was a hole in the roof
   c) there was an artificial light
   d) the treasure shone brightly.

B Answer in complete sentences.

1. Why do you think Ali Baba chose that particular tree to hide in?
2. Explain why he thought the men were thieves.
3. Explain how the door opened and closed.
4. Describe in your own words what Ali Baba found in the cave.
5. What risks did Ali Baba take by entering the cave?

C Answer in more than one sentence.
What sort of person do you think Ali Baba is? What makes you think so?

Clauses

A **clause** is a group of words which **contains a verb**. We can add a clause to a simple sentence to make a longer, more interesting sentence.

Ali Baba hid in a tree.

Ali Baba hid in a tree **because he thought the men were thieves.**

A Copy and complete these sentences with a suitable **clause**.

until they had disappeared from sight
which was overhung by a steep rock

who seemed to be the captain
showing him the most wonderful treasures

approaching him very fast
going back the same way they had come

1. Ali Baba saw a cloud of dust …
2. He climbed a tree …
3. The man … went up to the rock.
4. The horsemen set off …
5. Ali Baba watched …
6. Bright light shone through a hole in the roof …

B Put these **clauses** in sentences of your own.
1. who was limping badly
2. which was barking loudly
3. whose arm was broken
4. before you go out
5. without hesitating for a moment
6. silently opening the door

C Add a **suitable clause** to each of these sentences.
1. He met a man.
2. She bought a picture.
3. He read a book.
4. They arrived late.
5. They swam in the sea.
6. The match was cancelled.

Writing your own traditional story

Read this traditional story, then write your own story using the ideas on page 66.

I Know What I'll Do

Many traditional tales have main characters who solve their problems by using their brains. This tale is from Turkey.

One day the *Hoca* fell asleep as he was jogging along the road on his little grey donkey. Seeing a fine chance for a joke, several of his students slipped up behind him and removed the worn saddlebag from his donkey's back. Then they waited to see what would happen.

When he arrived at his stable door, the Hoca dismounted and reached out to remove the saddlebag. To his astonishment, it had disappeared entirely. The Hoca rubbed his eyes and looked again, but the saddlebag was nowhere to be seen.

The next day he encountered several of his students on the street that ran past the public fountain. "Boys," said he, "my saddlebag is gone. If you don't bring it back to me, I know what *I'll* do …" and he muttered something under his breath.

The boys looked at one another in dismay. Their prank had suddenly become a serious matter. In no time at all, they brought the missing saddlebag and presented it to the Hoca.

Thanking them, the Hoca installed it in its rightful place on the back of his little donkey, and he was about to ride away when one of the boys could contain his curiosity no longer. "I say, Hoca *effendi*," he began, "what were you going to do if we did not return the saddlebag?"

"Ah," answered the Hoca mildly, "I have at home a piece of old carpet. If you had not returned the saddlebag, I should have had to make another one."

From *Turkish Folk-Tales* retold by Barbara K. Walker

Write your own traditional story. Here are some ideas to think about.

- A poor person finds hidden treasure.
- A thief is tricked into returning stolen goods.
- A lazy person is tricked into doing some work.
- A man pretends to have a magic hat and sells it to someone else for a high price.

Make up a surprise ending!

- Decide who you are writing the story for. Plan your story for that audience.
- Make up incidents you expect your audience will enjoy.
- Use interesting words your audience will understand and find interesting.
- When you have written your story, review and edit it with your audience in mind.
- Write a final draft.

Everyday expressions

These **everyday expressions** do not mean what they appear to mean.
They are **metaphors**, speaking about something as if it were something else.

armed to the teeth
(completely armed)

carried away
(highly excited)

under a cloud
(in trouble)

A Match each **everyday expression** to its meaning.

> brave   the ordinary person
>
> unhappy   nothing to do
>
> useless   good enough

1. at a loose end
2. the man in the street
3. good for nothing
4. down in the mouth
5. lion-hearted
6. up to the mark

B Use each **expression** in **A** in a sentence of your own to show its meaning.

C Explain the **meaning** of these **expressions**.
1. heavy-eyed
2. in the same boat
3. hard up
4. hard of hearing
5. pull someone's leg
6. turn over a new leaf
7. mind your 'ps' and 'qs'
8. turn the tables

D Use each **expression** in **C** in a sentence of your own.

Unit 21

Moonlight and Candlelight

Wriggly is a young Guyanese girl. She finds a twenty-five cent silver coin.
It is the first time she has found so much money.

Wriggly gripped the cold coin tightly in her fist, her fingers gently searching out all the little ridges that ran around it. Her mind flashed from sugarcakes to toffee to red iced fruities, and finally came to rest on something her mother was always telling her to keep, a puzzling-tin, to save up her money in.

Thoughts of a puzzling-tin, brimming with money, were full in Wriggly's head as she dropped her vine-rope on the beach and began to head back home. Her heart warmed whenever she felt the hard coin in her pocket. But it was getting late and Wriggly could not see a single other person in sight.

Wriggly quickened her footsteps. She was just passing another dark clump of courida trees when she looked up and saw a huge orange ball staring down at her from between the trees. Wriggly gasped at the sight and it was some moments before she realized it was the moon.

But it was so big and shone with such a strange glow that Wriggly just stood there staring at it. She had never seen the moon like that before. And as Wriggly gazed at it she also noticed a funny pinkish tint about the skies and a queer silence about the trees and the shore.

Now, Wriggly's imagination was such that it wasn't long before she began to put two and two together, her heart pounding all the while. Perhaps the moon was a sign. A sign that the world was going to end. Her Sunday School teacher had told her all about it. That one day the world would end and Jesus and his angels would burst through the skies, and a loud trumpet would be sounded.

Wriggly became cold at the thought of it, and the next moment she was running, faster than the speed of lightning, her heart doing a mad somersault within her chest, her feet almost tripping her up in their haste. Wriggly never stopped running until she came to the back steps of their home. There, she sat down panting and began to pray. "Please God, forgive me for all the bad things I've done and please save me and let me go up to heaven. Please save my mother and father and all my friends. Please, please, please."

From *Trust You Wriggly* by Grace Nichols

Wriggly and the big orange moon

Read the passage, then answer each question.

A Choose the answer which tells what the story really says.
1. Wriggly decided to:
   a) spend the coin on sugarcakes   **b)** save the coin
   c) buy red iced fruities   **d)** buy a puzzling-tin.
2. The coin:
   a) warmed her heart
   b) made her afraid that there was no one else around
   c) made her gasp   **d)** caused her heart to pound.
3. The moon was unusual because:
   a) it was so big   **b)** it shone with a strange glow
   c) there was a pinkish tint in the skies
   d) all of the above.
4. Wriggly thought that the moon was a sign that the world
   was going to end, because:
   a) a loud trumpet had sounded
   b) she had found a coin which did not belong to her
   c) her Sunday School teacher had told her about it
   d) angels had burst through the skies.
5. This thought made her
   a) do mad somersaults   **b)** gasp
   c) run home   **d)** all of the above.

B Answer in complete sentences.
1. Explain how Wriggly felt when she found the coin.
2. Why do you think she kept feeling the coin?
3. How did seeing the moon change the way she felt?
4. How did she feel at the end of the extract?
5. What sort of person do you think Wriggly is? Give reasons for your answer.

C Answer in more than one sentence.
  How might these events change Wriggly's decision on how she will use the money? What makes you think so?

Prepositions

A **preposition** is a word which **links** two nouns or pronouns.

> Wriggly put the coin **in** her pocket.
> Clouds blew **across** the sky.

A Copy and complete these sentences with a suitable **preposition**.

in   on   up   down   between through   across   below

1. She climbed _____ the steep path.
2. The sea was far _____ her.
3. He fell _____ the stairs.
4. He looked _____ the telescope.
5. The cat ran _____ the house.
6. They tied a rope _____ the two trees.
7. He put the pie _____ a plate.
8. The bull chased him _____ the field.

B Change the meaning of these sentences by changing the underlined **preposition**.
1. He ran <u>through</u> the garden.
2. She went <u>up</u> the steps.
3. The road went <u>under</u> the bridge.
4. She parked <u>in front of</u> the house.
5. The <u>top of</u> the mountain was <u>below</u> the clouds.
6. He walked <u>from</u> the church.
7. He placed the ladder <u>against</u> the wall.
8. Mina arrived <u>after</u> Sangita.

C Use each **preposition** in a sentence of your own.
1. above   2. under   3. around
4. over   5. behind   6. along
7. towards   8. beyond

Continuing the story of Wriggly

A Write about what might happen next in the story.
Write in the style of the author.

- Do you think the big orange moon is a sign that the world is about to end?

- How will Wriggly use the money she found?

- What will her parents say?

- How will it all end?

Plan your story in three or four paragraphs.

Verb endings

Look at how these verbs add **endings**.

hope + **ed** = hoped	live + **ed** = lived	move + **ing** = moving
live + **ing** = living	sip+ **ed** = sipped	chop + **ed** = chopped
tap + **ing** = tapping	bat + **ing** = batting	

A Copy and complete these spelling rules.
1. Verbs ending in **e** _____ before adding -**ed** or -**ing**.
2. One-syllable verbs with a short vowel _____ before adding -**ed** or -**ing**.

B Add -**ed** to these words. Use each one in a sentence.
1. trip
2. smile
3. stare
4. hug
5. scrape
6. type
7. step
8. plug

C Add -**ing** to these words.
Use each one in a sentence.
1. celebrate
2. welcome
3. star
4. prepare
5. hop
6. skip
7. tease
8. stare
9. mop
10. scrape

Unit 22

Getting Granny's Glasses

Granny needs new glasses but she lives at least two day's journey from the nearest eye-hospital.

Granny could hear the distant roar of the river, and smell the pine needles beneath her feet, and feel the presence of her grandson, Mani; but she couldn't see the river or the trees; and of her grandson she could only make out his fuzzy hair, and sometimes, when he was very close, his blackberry eyes and the gleam of his teeth when he smiled.

Granny wore a pair of old glasses; she'd been wearing them for well over ten years, but her eyes had grown steadily weaker, and the glasses had grown older and were now scratched and spotted, and there was very little she could see through them. Still, they were better than nothing. Without them, everything was just a topsy-turvy blur. Of course Granny knew her way about the house and the fields, and on a clear day she could see the mountains – the mighty Himalayan snow-peaks – striding away into the sky; but it was felt by Mani and his father that it was high time Granny had her eyes tested and got herself new glasses.

"Well, you know we can't get them in the village," said Granny.

Mani (pronounced "money") said: "You'll have to go to the eye-hospital in Mussoorie. That's the nearest town."

"But that's a two-day journey," protested Granny. "First I'd have to walk to Nain market, twelve miles at least, spend the night there at your uncle's place, and then catch a bus for the rest of the journey! You know how I hate buses. And its ten years since I walked all the way to Mussoorie. That was when I had *these* glasses made."

"Well, it's still there," said Mani's father.

"What is?"

"Mussoorie."

"And the eye-hospital?"

"That too."

"Well, my eyes are not too bad, really," said Granny, looking for excuses. She did not feel like going far from the village; in particular she did not want to be parted from Mani. He was eleven and quite capable of looking after himself, but Granny had brought him up ever since his mother had died when he was only a year old. She was his *Nani* (maternal grandmother), and had cared for boy and father, and cows and hens and household all these years, with great energy and devotion. Even her failing eyesight hadn't prevented her from milking cows or preparing meals or harvesting the corn.

From *Getting Granny's Glasses* by Ruskin Bond

Day 1

Granny's old glasses

Read the passage, then answer each question.

A Choose the answer which tells what the story really says.
1. Through her glasses Granny could see:
   a) nothing at all   b) the distant river
   c) a topsy-turvy blur   d) very little.
2. She lived:
   a) at Mussoorie   b) in a village
   c) at the peak of a Himalayan mountain
   d) near Nain market.
3. She hated:
   a) buses   b) her glasses
   c) Mani   d) walking.
4. Mani was:
   a) nine b)   ten
   c) eleven   d) twelve.
5. Her failing eyesight prevented her from:
   a) milking cows   b) seeing Mani clearly
   c) preparing meals   d) all of the above.

B Answer in complete sentences.
1. How well do you think Granny got on with Mani and his father? What makes you think so?
2. Explain why Granny could not see properly.
3. Why did Granny say, "My eyes are not too bad, really"?
4. Explain why it was difficult for her to get new glasses.
5. What do you think will happen next? What makes you think so?

C Answer in more than one sentence.

What kind of person do you think Granny is? What makes you think so?

Day 2

Spelling: using prefixes and suffixes

Say these words to yourself:

hat hate   hop hope   pin pine

Notice that the **e** changes the sound of the vowel: **hop** becomes **hope.** We call this a **modifying e,** but sometimes it is known as a **magic e** because it changes the sound.

Work out for yourself the spelling rule for adding a **suffix** to a word ending in a **modifying, or magic, e.**

hope + ful = hopeful   love + ly = lovely

A Copy and complete this spelling rule.

Words ending in a **modifying, or magic, e**

_____.

B Make a new word from these words by adding **-ful**, **-ly** or **-less**.
1. care   2. lone   3. bone   4. fine   5. rude
6. like   7. brave   8. hate   9. spite   10. complete

These prefixes give a word its opposite meaning: **in-, im-, il-, ir-.**

   complete **in**complete   probable **im**probable

C Add one of these prefixes to each word below.

   in-   im-   il-   ir-

1. patient   2. expensive   3. responsible
4. possible   5. legal   6. curable   7. regular
8. capable   9. perfect   10. legible

D Use each word you made in **B** in a sentence of your own.

E Choose five of the words you made in **C** and use each in a sentence of your own.

Granny's problem

A Write about Granny's problem. Plan your writing in four or five paragraphs.

- Explain why Granny has trouble seeing.

- Explain the difficulties she faces in getting new glasses.

- What do you think she should do?

- How might she be persuaded to go to the eye hospital?

- How might she be helped to get there?

B Imagine you are Mani. Write a letter to a friend, about Granny and her problem, giving your point of view.

S

Day 5

The apostrophe for possession

We can use an apostrophe to show that something belongs to someone.

The **glasses of Granny** → **Granny's glasses**.

The apostrophe is used to show that the glasses belong to Granny.

> Always put the apostrophe **straight after the owner**, whether singular or plural, e.g. the pen of the teacher – the teacher's pen; the cars of the teachers – the teachers' cars.

A Rewrite these using **apostrophes**. The first one has been done for you.
1. the bike of Gill   *Gill's bike*
2. the house of Mr Smith
3. the money of Omar
4. the helmet of the policeman
5. the garden of Mrs Jones
6. the coats of the ladies
7. the barking of the dogs
8. the chimes of the clocks

B Copy these sentences. Add **apostrophes** where necessary.
1. Manis mother was her grandmothers daughter.
2. Mani is Grannys grandson and his fathers son.
3. Johns book is on the teachers desk.
4. We went out in Dads car with our uncles dog.
5. We took Toms bat and Pats football.
6. Mrs Kings dog chased Mr James dog into Ms Simmons garden.
7. The owls hooting disturbed the babies sleep.

C Put each of the **apostrophe** forms you made in **A** in a sentence of your own.

The Banana Machine

Grandfather Michael has gambled away half of his banana plantation.

Now there were some neighbours who would have laughed and said: "No worry. We'd never take away your land." But the man who had won the land was not like that. He took up the piece of paper, folded it carefully, and put it in his pocket. Then he said: "That's just fine, then. Give me the deeds to the land tomorrow morning."

Grandfather Michael looked his neighbour in the eye and nodded.

"I promised, and so I will," he said. "I'll be over at your place just after eight."

And so it was that half the banana plantation was lost, and when it passed to Aunt Bat after Grandfather Michael died it was hardly large enough to keep one family.

Because the plantation was so small, Aunt Bat did most of the work, and she was helped by Patty and Mike. Patty and Mike had to go to school, though, and could only help afterwards. So everybody was always busy looking after the trees and trying to make sure the bananas grew as big and healthy as possible.

But even with all this hard work, things were not going well.

"I wish we could get more money for our bananas," sighed Aunt Bat when she returned from the fruit market in nearby Port Antonio. "If it goes on like this, I'm afraid we'll have to sell the plantation. I could get a job in town, I suppose. I know people down there who would give me work."

"But we can't sell this place," protested Patty. "We've always lived here! We've always grown bananas!"

Aunt Bat shook her head.

"If the price they pay for bananas gets much lower," she said, "it won't be worth growing them any more. We might as well give up."

From *The Banana Machine* by Alexander McCall Smith

Half the plantation is lost

Read the passage, then answer each question.

A Choose the answer which tells what the story really says.

1. Half of the plantation was lost because:
   a) Grandfather Michael gambled it away
   b) there was a tropical storm
   c) Grandfather Michael gave it away
   d) none of the above.
2. Half of the plantation was:
   a) won by Aunt Bat
   b) lost by Aunt Bat
   c) given to Aunt Bat
   d) left to Aunt Bat when Grandfather Michael died.

3. Things were not going well at the plantation because:
   a) it was so small
   b) Aunt Bat did most of the work
   c) the price paid for bananas was too low
   d) Patty and Mike could help only after school.
4. The bananas were sold:
   a) in the fruit market
   b) in Port Antonio
   c) at a low price
   d) all of the above.
5. Aunt Bat said they might as well give up:
   a) because the price of bananas was too low
   b) if the price of bananas went any lower
   c) because she could get a job in town
   d) because they had always grown bananas.

B Answer in complete sentences.
1. The man who won the land put a piece of paper in his pocket. What do you think it was? What makes you think so?
2. Explain how the family tried to cope with the work.
3. What was the biggest problem they faced?
4. What sort of person do you think Grandfather Michael was? Give reasons for your answer.
5. What do you think will happen next? What makes you think so?

C Answer in more than one sentence.

Do you think the neighbour was right to take the plantation? Explain your answer.

Clauses

In a sentence with more than one clause, one of them is usually the **main clause.**

A main clause can stand on its own without another clause.

Because the plantation was so small, **Aunt Bat did most of the work.**

The **main clause** is **Aunt Bat did most of the work**. This is because it makes sense on its own.

The clause **because the plantation was so small** does not make sense on its own, and so cannot be the main clause.

Commas usually separate the **main clause** from other clauses.

A Copy these sentences. Underline the **main clause**.
1. If it goes on like this, we will have to sell the plantation.
2. He was very happy, because he passed the test.
3. Though he tried his best to lift it, the suitcase was too heavy.
4. If you finish your work, you can go out.
5. He jumped out of bed when the alarm went off.
6. She started work as soon as she arrived.

B Make a sentence by adding a **main clause** to each of these clauses.
1. when I grow up
2. if I were strong enough
3. after school is over
4. as I was going home
5. until it got too dark
6. before we finished
7. unless it rains
8. if his cold gets much worse

74

Writing

A Imagine you are Patty. Write a letter to a friend explaining how Grandfather Michael lost half his plantation and the problems that it has caused Aunt Bat. Tell your friend what you think and how you feel about your situation.

B What do you think will happen next? Continue the story in the style of the author.

More about clauses

These two sentences can be joined into a single sentence:

I know people in town. They would give me work.

<u>I know people in town</u> who would give me work.

The main clause in the second sentence is underlined.

A Join these sentences. Choose a suitable **joining word**. Underline the main clause.

**unless though after
where before until**

1. He read the book. He went to bed.
2. She sang sweetly. She did not win the competition.
3. Your work improves. You cannot play with your friends.
4. You can't come with me. You tidy yourself up.
5. He had a cup of coffee. He went shopping.
6. He planted the tree. The other one had died.

B Join these sentences. Underline the **main clause**.
1. When ... Grandfather Michael died. The plantation passed to Aunt Bat.
2. Although ... The food is good. It is not as good as it used to be.
3. If ... She will help me. I will help her.
4. He couldn't play in the match. He hurt his leg.
5. I'll help you. I have finished this job.
6. We won't be able to go out. It stops raining.

C Make a sentence by adding a **main clause** to each of these clauses.
1. when Jake comes
2. until the bell goes
3. who does odd jobs for us
4. which barks at strangers
5. whenever you like
6. as soon as you have finished
7. who never eats meat
8. as I was crossing the bridge
9. although he said I couldn't
10. if you fall off your bike
11. because it's too cold
12. even though I did my best

Akimbo and the Crocodile Man

Akimbo is a young African boy who lives on a game reserve. John is the game ranger who teaches him about the animals.

The river bank seemed deserted for the time being, although Akimbo knew well that this did not mean that there were no crocodiles about.

They had negotiated several bends in the river when they came across the island. It was at a point where the river broadened out considerably and was fairly shallow in parts. The island was not big, but supported a fair amount of vegetation, including a clump of tall heavy-leafed trees. John was delighted to have found it, and quickly paddled the boat over to a muddy beach about half way along one side.

They beached the boat and got out to explore. John wanted to see if there were any sandy places which might be used by crocodiles for hatching.

Akimbo wanted to walk from one end to the other, just to see what it was like.

"Be careful of snakes," John warned as Akimbo made his way up to the ridge that ran through the middle of the island. "Have a look round, and then come back here."

Akimbo climbed up to the top of the ridge and looked down. John had left the boat on the muddy beach and was making his way through the reeds, looking for signs of crocodiles.

Akimbo turned away and began his exploration of the island. There was not much to see, though. There were no animals, although he thought he saw monkeys in a tree at one point, and there were no interesting rocks or caves. All in all, he thought, as he reached the tip of the island and turned back, it's a boring place.

It was then that he heard the cry. It was a shout, a yell, and it came from the other end of the island. Akimbo stopped in his tracks and listened, but all he heard was the screeching of cicadas and the sound of calling birds.

Then there was another cry, and this time Akimbo knew.

Running wildly, blinding, his heart pumping fear into his limbs, Akimbo crashed through the undergrowth. It took only a few minutes, and he was there, at the point of the ridge from which he had set out. And there below him, he saw John, half in the water and half out, struggling and calling out in a mass of foaming water.

From *Akimbo and the Crocodile Man* by Alexander McCall Smith

Day 1 Akimbo and John explore

Read the passage, then answer each question.

A Choose the answer which tells what the story really says.

1. The island:
   a) seemed deserted
   b) supported a fair amount of vegetation
   c) broadened out considerably
   d) was full of crocodiles.
2. Akimbo:
   a) was delighted to have found the island
   b) left the boat on the beach
   c) looked for signs of crocodiles
   d) climbed to the top of the ridge.

3. John warned Akimbo to be careful of:
   a) crocodiles   b) sandy places
   c) snakes   d) monkeys.
4. Akimbo thought that the island was:
   a) boring   b) interesting
   c) dangerous   d) big.
5. He heard:
   a) a yell
   b) the screeching of cicadas
   c) the sound of calling birds
   d) all of the above.

B Answer in complete sentences.

1. How can you tell that it was not the first time Akimbo had been on the river?
2. Why do you think John was called "the crocodile man"?
3. What were they looking for on the island? What makes you think so?
4. Describe the island in your own words.
5. How can you tell that the island was not big?

C Answer in more than one sentence.

What do think has happened to John? What makes you think so? What might happen next?

Day 2 Combining sentences

These three sentences can be combined into a single sentence.

He heard a cry. It was a shout. It came from the other end of the island.

He heard a cry, which was a shout, coming from the other end of the island.

A Combine each set of three sentences into a single sentence.

1. He was climbing a tree. He fell. He was not hurt.
2. She was coming out of the shop. She saw her friend. Her friend was on a bike.
3. Ali went out early. He went into the wood. He liked listening to the birdsong.
4. He unlocked the door. He still couldn't open it. The door was jammed.
5. She was woken up. The dog jumped on the bed. It licked her face.
6. Mum was happy. Dad was happy. Carly had learned to swim.

B Do the same with these. Combine each set of three sentences into a single sentence.

1. Akimbo watched the river bank. It seemed deserted. He knew this did not mean there were no crocodiles.
2. He got there early. He started work. He finished before the others arrived.
3. We have a cat. It is very big. It chases dogs.
4. He didn't think he would be able to do it. He took a long run. He jumped across the stream.
5. He took a shower. He had his breakfast. He dashed to work.
6. She was disappointed. She couldn't play netball. She had to go to the dentist.

To the rescue!

What do you think has happened to John, the crocodile man? What can Akimbo do to help? How dangerous might this be?

Continue the story saying how Akimbo rescues John and what happens after that. Write in the style of the author.

Plan your story in four paragraphs.

Paragraph 1: Akimbo finds John.

Paragraph 2: Akimbo rescues John.

Paragraph 3: how they get off the island to safety.

Paragraph 4: how it all ends.

W

Day 5

Using a dictionary

Dictionaries are useful for checking spellings and for finding the meanings of words.

A Some of these words are spelt correctly, but others are not. Use a dictionary to check each spelling. Write the correct spelling for each word.
1. vegitation
2. strugle
3. screech
4. muddy
5. crocadile
6. explore
7. minite
8. negociate

B Copy and complete these sentences by choosing the best word. Use a dictionary to check your answers.
1. "Help!," he _____. (exclaimed, yelled, examined)
2. She waited _____. (pathetically, patiently, patently)
3. The goat was _____ to a post. (bound, tethered, knotted)
4. He replied _____ to her letter. (promptly, hastily, rapidly)
5. He was a _____ because he wasted his money. (miser, hoarder, spendthrift)
6. She looked for her name on the _____. (roster, rooster, rostrum)

C Write your own definition for each of these words. Check your answers with a dictionary.
1. several
2. delighted
3. explore
4. screech
5. blindly
6. deserted
7. island
8. vegetation
9. track
10. beach

Learn the correct spelling of each word in **A**. Use the **Look**, **Say**, **Cover**, **Write**, **Check** strategy.

In My Opinion

What you read in newspapers may not always be what it seems.

Labour lead in opinion poll

Liberal gains, Labour losses

Results of opinion poll		
Labour	34%	(47%)
Conservatives	33%	(19%)
Liberal	21%	(17%)
Others	9%	(13%)
Don't know	3%	(4%)
Last month's figures in brackets.		

Massive swing to Conservatives

Pupils happy to wear school uniform

Schoolchildren gave the thumbs up to school uniform in today's *Evening News* survey.

"I'm happy to wear school uniform," declared schoolgirl Sophie Robinson. Jake Briggs told us he liked school uniform. After all the recent debate on the subject Hayley Jones summed up current feeling among schoolchildren: "It's all right to wear school uniform." Only a few children disagreed with her.

It's all right to wear school uniform if everyone else is wearing it.
Hayley Jones

I like school uniform – on other people!
Jake Briggs

I'm happy to wear school uniform? I don't think so!
Sophie Robinson

Dear Editor,

Something must be done about vandalism in this town. Are we expected to ignore the smashed bus shelters, graffiti and litter? Every right-minded person must agree that this has got to stop. But has the council done anything? No!

Naturally we can't expect the problem to be solved overnight. Yet nobody but a complete idiot would go on spending public money year after year replacing things only to have them smashed again. Who wants to see his council tax wasted in this way? What kind of people are we if we stand by and watch our beloved town be wrecked?

It surely wouldn't be very difficult to begin the fight back, but the real truth is the council is just too frightened.

Disgusted pensioner

Newspaper cuttings

Read the cuttings, then answer each question.

A Choose the answer which tells what the cuttings really say.
1. Jake Briggs:
   a) likes school uniform
   b) likes other people to wear school uniform
   c) is happy to wear school uniform
   d) agrees with Sophie Robinson.

2. The opinion poll shows that:
   a) Labour is in the lead
   b) the positions are unchanged from the previous month
   c) some people don't know which party they would vote for
   d) all of the above.
3. The disgusted pensioner thinks the council:
   a) has done nothing to prevent vandalism
   b) should spend money replacing things which have been smashed
   c) should waste his council tax   **d)** none of the above.
4. Koldban is:
   a) a new cough medicine **b)** made by Barratt and Crawford
   c) advertised on TV   **d)** a treatment for colds.

B Answer in complete sentences.
1. Explain why the report on school uniform is misleading.
2. Why do you think the reporter has misquoted people?
3. How can all the headlines in the political opinion poll be true?
4. Pick out words and phrases which the pensioner has used to persuade the reader.
5. Why do you think the Koldban advertisement is designed to look like a news report?

C Answer in more than one sentence.
Do you think Koldban is really the amazing breakthrough it claims to be? What makes you think so?

Persuasive devices

Persuasive devices are ways in which a writer deliberately sets out to persuade us to accept his point of view.

Bias and half-truths

Bias means **favouring** one side **unfairly**. A biased writer often uses half-truths by deliberately selecting only the facts which support his argument.

What does the reporter on school uniforms want us to believe?
How has he deliberately distorted the words of the children?

Write your own unbiased report based on the children's opinions about school uniform.

Disguising opinion as fact

Many advertisements disguise opinions as facts. Bennet and Crawford claim that Koldban is an amazing breakthrough in cold treatment, but is it really a breakthrough? Who says so? Do most people think it a breakthrough, or just Bennet and Crawford? Do Bennet and Crawford really believe it themselves, or is it just that they would like us to believe it?

Make a list of **opinions** disguised as facts from the Koldban advertisement.
Begin like this: 1. *an amazing breakthrough*

Make a list of the **facts** in the Koldban advertisement.

Write your own factual report about Koldban.
Begin like this: *Bennet and Crawford have a new product called Koldban, which they claim ...*

Writing a letter to a newspaper

Write a letter to a newspaper on one of these subjects:

● vandalism

● school uniform

● an issue you feel strongly about.

● Plan your letter in paragraphs.

Paragraph 1: introduce your subject and state your point of view.

Paragraph 2: explain your reasons for thinking that way.

Paragraph 3: suggest what action you would like to see taken.

● Edit your letter carefully.

● Copy it out neatly.

Day 5

Abbreviations

Some words, phrases and names of companies are often written, or spoken of, in the **shortened form** known as **abbreviations**.

BBC – British Broadcasting Corporation   **km** – kilometre
DIY – do-it-yourself

A What do these abbreviations stand for?
1. CD   2. USA   3. DJ   4. FA
5. approx   6. mph   7. e.g.   8. etc

B Write the abbreviations for these.
1. television
2. Independent Television
3. random access memory
4. video cassette recorder
5. water closet
6. post office
7. value added tax
8. centimetre
9. Youth Hostel Association
10. Amateur Athletic Association

C What do these abbreviations stand for? Use a dictionary to help you.
1. CID   2. mm   3. g   4. St   5. PC
6. WPC   7. am   8. pm   9. PM   10. p
11. P   12. VIP   13. UFO   14. UN

D Collect abbreviations from your reading. Sort them under these headings: **single words**; **phrases**; **names of companies**, etc.

Riches of the Rainforest

The rainforests are scattered in a broad band across the Equator, but they are disappearing at an alarming rate.

Think of Aladdin's Cave, full of chests brimming with multicoloured jewels, riches beyond your wildest dreams … To someone who studies plants or insects, animals or birds, the tropical rainforests of the world are one big Aladdin's Cave. Nowhere else is there such a rich mixture of life, nowhere else contains so many secrets we have yet to discover, secrets that might cure illnesses or prevent disease, or perhaps provide new sources of food.

With so much to offer, it is an international disaster that the rainforests are being "eaten up" at such an alarming rate. Whether it is Central and South America, Africa, or countries like the Philippines and Malaysia in the Far East, the story is the same. Rainforests are being destroyed to make way for "civilized" man to grow crops, to provide timber, to "develop" the land. About half the world's rainforest has already gone. An area the size of England, Scotland and Wales goes up in smoke every year.

Rainforest life

We are losing species at an astonishing rate because of the destruction of the rainforests. About 50 a day, or one every half hour or so, disappears off the face of the earth forever. Each one plays some part in the balance of nature in the rainforest. And while species are disappearing, we might be losing forever cures for crippling diseases.

Rainforest people

There are thought to be about 200 million tribal people living in the rainforests.

They know how to harvest the rainforests, which plants can be eaten, and which ones are medicines. From Borneo to Brazil, their lands are in danger.

Iaulapiti Indians from Brazil

Flowers and plants

Thanks to a little rosy periwinkle found in Madagascar, nearly all children now recover from the blood disease, leukaemia. Rainforest plants are like a chemist's counter and thousands of them contain things that are or can be used in medicines. Beautiful rare orchids are traded, but they belong in the tropics as much as ivory belongs to an elephant.

Animals and birds

The thick layers of vegetation between the forest floor and the treetops provide a choice of habitats for the teeming wildlife of the rainforests. Most creatures live in the canopy, just below the treetops. Some exotic animals – like the komodo dragon and the huge atlas moth – are unique to the rainforest. Some are very rare and endangered, like the lemurs of Madagascar and the mountain gorillas of Rwanda. About half of all the species in the world live in rainforests.

From *The Blue Peter Green Book* by Lewis Bronze, Nick Heathcote and Peter Brown

Day 1

An Aladdin's cave

Read the passage, then answer each question.

A Choose the answer which tells what the text really says.

1. The tropical rainforests of the world are:
   a) a cave full of jewels
   b) an area the size of England, Scotland and Wales
   c) being "eaten up" at an alarming rate
   d) in the Far East.

2. Rainforest people:
   a) are thought to live in the rainforest
   b) are about 200 million in number
   c) are dangerous   d) all of the above.

3. The rosy periwinkle:
   a) has helped cure a children's blood disease
   b) belongs in the tropics
   c) is like a chemist's counter   d) belongs to an elephant.

4. Most rainforest creatures live:
   a) on the forest floor
   b) in thick layers of vegetation between the forest floor and the treetops
   c) in the canopy, just below the treetops
   d) in Madagascar.

5. The main idea of the text is that:
   a) large areas of the rainforest are destroyed every year
   b) plants which might provide new medicines are being destroyed
   c) animal species are being lost at an astonishing rate
   d) all of the above.

B Answer in complete sentences.

1. In what way are the rainforests like one big Aladdin's Cave?
2. Why are the rainforests being destroyed?
3. Explain how the knowledge of the rainforest peoples could help everyone.
4. Why are the plants of the rainforest important?
5. Explain how the destruction of the rainforest endangers rare animals.

C Answer in more than one sentence.
   Why do you think the destruction of the rainforest is an international disaster?

Day 2

Changing nouns and verbs

Some **verbs** can be changed **to nouns** by adding a **suffix**.

collect → collect**ion**   perform → perform**ance**

Some **nouns** can be changed **into verbs** by adding a **suffix**.

advertisement → advert**ise**   solid → solid**ify**

A Change these **verbs into nouns** by adding one of these suffixes.

   -ment -ance -ion -y

1. develop   2. arrange
3. prevent   4. allow
5. recover   6. impress
7. appear   8. reflect

B Change these **verbs into nouns**. You may have to change the spelling before adding one of these suffixes.

   -ion   -y   -al   -ism

1. baptise   2. destroy
3. produce   4. refuse
5. pollute   6. discover
7. criticise 8. arrive

C Change these **nouns into verbs** by adding one of the suffixes below. Make any other changes necessary.

   -ise -ify -en

1. recognition   2. glory
3. terror   4. liquid
5. horror   6. moisture
7. strength   8. advice
9. appetite   10. apology

Preparing an argument

Use the information in the passage on page 82 to make notes under these headings.

- **Why rainforests are being destroyed**
- **The effect on people, plants and animals**
- **What man is losing because of the destruction**

Do it like this:

Why rainforests are being destroyed

Rainforests destroyed to: grow crops, cut timber, develop land.

Use your notes to write an argument to persuade others of the need to stop the destruction of the rainforests.

Designing a poster

Use your notes to design a poster drawing the public's attention to the destruction of the rainforest. Make clear what is happening, and why it is an international disaster.

- Think of an eye-catching slogan.
- Choose a strong design.
- Make your lettering bold and easy to read.
- Include all the important information, but don't use more words than necessary.

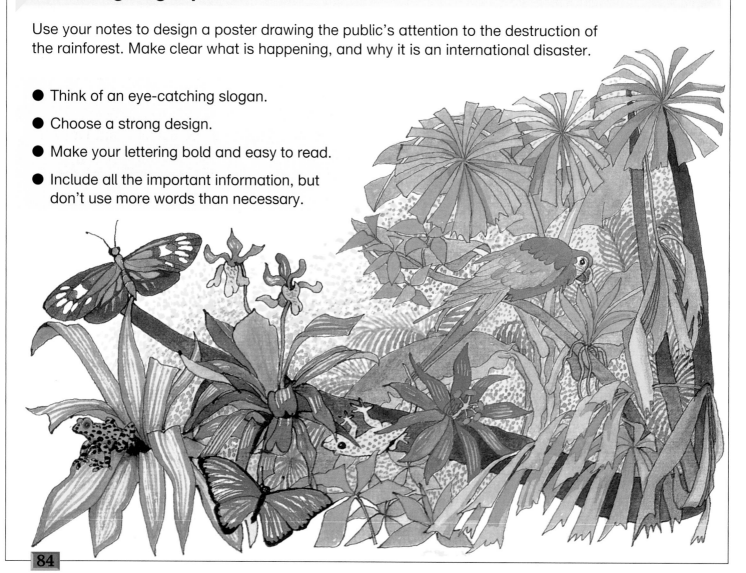

Protecting Species

All species rely on other species to survive. If just one species dies then many others may suffer.

Whales have been hunted, for food and other products, for thousands of years. But it wasn't until the 1870s that the mass slaughter of whales began, eventually threatening their existence. The invention of the grenade harpoon and the introduction of fast catcher boats, armed with bow-mounted cannons, meant whalers had much more efficient "killing machines". Now, even the giant blue whale, weighing up to 180 tonnes and 31 m long, fell victim.

Harpoon used in whale hunting

Each blue whale produced up to 30 tonnes of oil and so quickly became the main target. In 1930, the peak year, 30 000 of these magnificent creatures were killed. Today, it's *estimated* that there are fewer than 1000 "blues" left in the southern hemisphere, against nearly a quarter of a million before large-scale whaling began. Hunting is now officially banned. Only Japan and Norway still kill whales, mainly fin, sperm and minke, for what they call "scientific" purposes!

Dolphins in danger

Dolphins, which have developed a special "friendship" with humans over the centuries, are also threatened by pollution and people. Thousands of dolphins are dying around Japan's coasts as hunters cash in on the shortage of whale meat caused by the whaling ban. At least 130 000 more dolphins die each year by drowning when they get caught in tuna fishermen's nets. In parts of the eastern Pacific Ocean, the number of spinner dolphins has fallen by more than 80% since 1959. Greenpeace says only *urgent* action will save dolphins from extinction.

From *The Blue Peter Green Book* by Lewis Bronze, Nick Heathcote and Peter Brown

A bottle-nosed dolphin teaches a diver an underwater trick or two in the Bahamas.

Day 1 Whales and dolphins in danger

Read the passage, then answer each question.

A Choose the answer which tells what the text really says.

1. Whales have been hunted:
   a) for hundreds of years
   b) for thousands of years
   c) since the 1870s
   d) since 1930.
2. The giant blue whale:
   a) weighs up to 30 tonnes
   b) is now extinct
   c) is up to 31m long
   d) all of the above.
3. Whales are still killed by:
   a) Greenpeace
   b) Japan and Norway
   c) dolphins
   d) fishermen's nets.
4. Hunters now hunt the dolphin because:
   a) of the shortage of whale meat
   b) they have a special "friendship" with them
   c) dolphins are threatened by pollution
   d) of urgent action by Greenpeace.

B Answer in complete sentences.

1. Explain why whales were killed in greater numbers after the 1870s.
2. Explain why people hunt whales and dolphins.
3. Why is the giant blue whale now close to extinction?
4. What danger, apart from hunting, do dolphins face from man?

C Answer in more than one sentence.

Why do you think it is wrong to hunt dolphins? Give reasons for your answer.

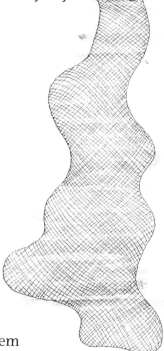

Day 2 Spelling

Look at these words:

try → tried	shy → shyly	fly → flying	fly → flies
century → centuries	story → stories	opportunity → opportunities	

A What is the general spelling rule for **adding a suffix** to words ending in **y**, preceded by a consonant? Give some exceptions to this rule.

B Make these words **plural**. Use each one in a sentence of your own.

1. enemy   2. responsibility
3. lorry   4. inquiry
5. ministry 6. family
7. ruby   8. baby

C Add one of these suffixes to each word.

   -ful -fully -ly -ing

1. hope   2. beauty
3. love   4. shop
5. shy   6. separate
7. make   8. accurate
9. grace   10. try

Use each word you have made in a sentence of your own.

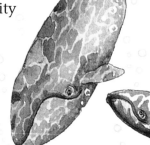

Writing a leaflet on an issue

Design a leaflet informing people about the need to protect whales and dolphins. It might be a single sheet, folded to make four pages, or two sheets folded to make eight pages.

The cover

Think of a slogan that people will remember. Make this the title of your leaflet.

Draw artwork or use a suitable photograph.

The text

● Explain the dangers whales and dolphins face. Offer evidence: facts and figures.

● Explain why these creatures must be protected.

● Explain what you think should be done.

● Explain how other people might help.

Make a rough of your leaflet first.

Then review and edit it for publication.

Finding out

We depend on many species of plants for food, clothes and medicines. Use information books and other sources to find out about them.
Make lists under these headings:
● **Food**
● **Clothes**
● **Medicine**
Choose one species. Explain how it is used.

Choral Poems

The poems in this unit are meant to be read aloud.

The Ceremonial Band

(To be said out loud by a chorus and solo voices)

The old King of Dorchester,
He had a little orchestra,
And never did you hear such a ceremonial band.
"Tootle-too," said the flute,
"Deed-a-reedle," said the fiddle,
For the fiddles and the flutes were the finest in the land.

The old King of Dorchester,
He had a little orchestra,
And never did you hear such a ceremonial band.
"Pump-a-rum," said the drum,
"Tootle-too," said the flute,
"Deed-a-reedle," said the fiddle,
For the fiddles and the flutes were the finest in the land.

The old King of Dorchester,
He had a little orchestra,
And never did you hear such a ceremonial band.
"Pickle-pee," said the fife,
"Pump-a-rum," said the drum,
"Tootle-too," said the flute,
"Deed-a-reedle," said the fiddle,
For the fiddles and the flutes were the finest in the land.

The old King of Dorchester,
He had a little orchestra,
And never did you hear such a ceremonial band.
"Zoomba-zoom," said the bass,
"Pickle-pee," said the fife,
"Pump-a-rum," said the drum,
"Tootle-too," said the flute,
"Deed-a-reedle," said the fiddle,
For the fiddles and the flutes were the finest in the land.

The old King of Dorchester,
He had a little orchestra,
And never did you hear such a ceremonial band.
"Pah-pa-rah," said the trumpet,
"Zoomba-zoom," said the bass,
"Pickle-pee," said the fife,
"Pump-a-rum," said the drum,
"Tootle-too," said the flute,
"Deed-a-reedle," said the fiddle,
For the fiddles and the flutes were the finest in the land,
Oh! the fiddles and the flutes were the finest in the land!

James Reeves

The Pow-wow Drum

Long black braids and silken shawls
Moving side by side where the eagle calls,
Answering the beat of the pow-wow drum
we come again
to dance again

Hey-a, Hey-a, Hey-a, Hey-a, Hey!
Hey-a, Hey-a, Hey-a, Hey-a, Hey!

Leave the dusty cities far behind,
Meet our brothers of the country with one mind,
Travelling from the east, north, south and west
we come again
to dance again

Chorus

Watching close the feet of lightning fly
Fancy dancers free underneath the sky,
Joining in the circle moving round and round
we come again
to dance again

Chorus

Women shining like the morning sun,
Children making rainbows as they laugh and run,
The old and young meeting like they did long ago
we come again
to dance again

Chorus

David Campbell

Day 1

All together now!

Read the poems, then answer each question.

A Choose the answer which tells what the poems really say.

1. "The Ceremonial Band" is intended to be read aloud by a chorus and:
   - **a)** two voices
   - **b)** five voices
   - **c)** six voices
   - **d)** none of the above.
2. The pow-wow drum brings people:
   - **a)** who are young and old
   - **b)** from all directions
   - **c)** from town and country
   - **d)** all of the above.
3. As the people dance:
   - **a)** the morning sun shines
   - **b)** lightning flashes
   - **c)** they move round and round
   - **d)** none of the above.
4. Both poems are about:
   - **a)** dancing
   - **b)** music
   - **c)** bands
   - **d)** singing.

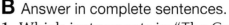

B Answer in complete sentences.

1. Which instruments in "The Ceremonial Band" would be best read aloud by
   - **a)** deep voices?
   - **b)** higher-pitched voices?
2. What does the word "chorus" mean in "The Pow-wow Drum"? What words does it stand for?
3. What do you think a pow-wow is?
4. What pictures does "The Pow-wow Drum" make in your mind?
5. Which poem do you like best? Give reasons for your answer.

C Answer in more than one sentence.

Which lines in each poem do you like best? Why?

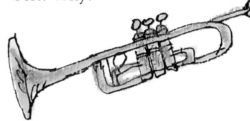

Day 2

All change

A Add **-er** and **-est** to these adjectives.

1. fine
2. long
3. dusty
4. close
5. young
6. shiny
7. fancy

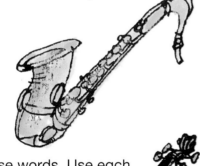

B Add **-ing** to these words. Use each one in a sentence of your own.

1. take
2. move
3. dance
4. make
5. shine
6. come

C Change these verbs into the **past tense**. Use each one in a sentence of your own.

1. joining
2. travel
3. singing
4. meet
5. shake
6. come
7. leaving

D Change these verbs to **nouns**. Use each noun in a sentence of your own.

1. move
2. meet
3. celebrate
4. perform
5. discuss
6. speak

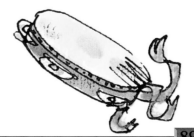

Your own choral poem

Write your own choral poem using either "**The Ceremonial Band**" or "**The Pow-wow Drum**" as a model.

Writing your poem

● Plan your poem for performance as a group with single voices.

● Experiment with repeating certain lines.

● Give your poem a strong rhythm.

● Imitate the sound of musical instruments, or the call of dancers.

Performing your poem

● Add notes to your finished poem to indicate how and by whom it should be read aloud. Do this with words, e.g. **All**, **Group 1**, **Group 2**, **Solo voice, softly, quickly,** etc.

● Perform your poem with other children. Make any necessary changes to the poem or the way it is performed.

Dialect and slang

● **Standard English** is the form of English we use when we need to be understood clearly in writing or speech.

● A **dialect** is a variety of English used in a particular region. Dialects have some words which are different from standard English, and the way words are put together is often different too. The poem "**Rap Connected**" is written in a West Indian dialect. It uses words and phrases such as: "riddim" for "rhythm", "de life dat we live" for "the life that we live".

● **Slang** is the name we give to the words and phrases we use informally amongst ourselves. Such words usually go out of fashion quite quickly. Slang is not used in formal writing or speech.

Collect examples of **dialect** words and phrases. Show how they are used and what they mean.

Make a dictionary of the **slang** words you use.

Railway Rhythms

Night Mail *was written for the soundtrack of a film about a train delivering the mail to Scotland.*

This is the night mail crossing the border,
Bringing the cheque and the postal order,
Letters for the rich, letters for the poor,
The shop at the corner and the girl next door.
Pulling up Beattock, a steady climb –
The gradient's against her, but she's on time.
Past cotton grass and moorland boulder,
Shovelling white steam over her shoulder,
Snorting noisily as she passes
Silent miles of wind-bent grasses.
Birds turn their heads as she approaches,
Stare from the bushes at her blank-faced coaches
Sheep-dogs cannot turn her course,
They slumber on with paws across.
In the farm she passes no one wakes,
But a jug in the bedroom gently shakes.

Dawn freshens, the climb is done.
Down towards Glasgow she descends
Towards the steam tugs yelping down the glade
of cranes,
Towards the fields of apparatus, the furnaces
Set on the dark plain like gigantic chessmen.
All Scotland waits for her:
In the dark glens, beside the pale-green lochs
Men long for news.

Letters of thanks, letters from banks,
Letters of joy from girl and boy,
Receipted bills and invitations
To inspect new stock or visit relations.
And applications for situations
And timid lovers' declarations
And gossip, gossip from all the nations,
News circumstantial, news financial,
Letters with holiday snaps to enlarge in,
Letters with faces scrawled in the margin,

Letters from uncles, cousins and aunts,
Letters to Scotland from the South of France,
Letters of condolence to Highlands and
Lowlands,
Notes from overseas to Hebrides;

Written on paper of every hue,
The pink, the violet, the white and the blue,
The chatty, the catty, the boring, adoring,
The cold and official and the heart's outpouring.
Clever, stupid, short and long,
The typed and the printed and the spelt
all wrong.

Thousands are still asleep
Dreaming of terrifying monsters,
Or of friendly tea beside the band at Cranston's
or Crawford's,
Asleep in working Glasgow, asleep in well-set
Edinburgh,
Asleep in granite Aberdeen,
They continue their dreams;
But shall wake soon and long for letters,
And none will hear the postman's knock
Without a quickening of the heart,
For who can bear to feel himself forgotten?

W.H. Auden

Day 1 Night mail

Read the poems, then answer each question.

A Choose the answer which tells what the poem really says.
1. The train is crossing the border into:
   a) Scotland **b)** Glasgow
   c) the South of France **d)** Edinburgh.
2. The giant chessmen in the poem are really:
   a) cranes **b)** furnaces
   c) birds **d)** letters.
3. At dawn the train:
   a) climbs the gradient **b)** begins to descend
   c) gently shakes a jug in a bedroom
   d) approaches Aberdeen.
4. The train is carrying:
   a) letters **b)** cheques and postal orders
   c) holiday snaps **d)** all of the above.
5. When the postman knocks people will:
   a) long for letters **b)** continue their dreams
   c) feel a quickening of the heart **d)** not hear his knock.

B Answer in complete sentences.
1. What do you think the word "hue" means? What makes you think so?
2. What does the rhythm of the poem remind you of?
3. Which verse has the most regular rhyme? What is its rhyming pattern?
4. How does the poem make you feel?
5. Which of the kinds of letter mentioned would you most like to receive? Why?

C Answer in more than one sentence.
Which are your favourite lines from the poem? Give reasons for your answer.

Day 2 The apostrophe

The **apostrophe** has two uses.
It shows that something belongs to someone.
> I hear the **postman's** knock.

It shows a missing letter in a word which has been shortened.
> **She's** on time.

A Copy these sentences. Add **apostrophes** where necessary.
1. I wont be long now. Im just reading Dads letter.
2. George couldnt open Mr Grahams front door.
3. Lets go to Jennys house on Saturday.
4. The postmans bag contained letters of thanks and Aunty Janes birthday card.
5. I cant read with Winstons trumpet and Lees drum making all that noise!

B Do the same with these sentences. Copy them and add **apostrophes** where necessary.
1. She borrowed Jos pen, Yasmins pencil and Helens book.
2. He couldnt wait to receive Sams invitation.
3. Why isnt this work finished? Is it that you cant or wont do it?
4. Its about time someone gave the dog its dinner.
5. I mightnt be able to borrow Andys football, but Michelles dads got one hed lend us.

C Rewrite these phrases with an **apostrophe**. The first one has been done for you.
1. the computer of Tom   *Tom's computer*
2. the car of the lady   3. the bags of the ladies
4. the house of Mr Barnes   5. the dogs of the farmers
6. the paws of the cat   7. the cries of the wolves
8. the brakes of the truck

D Use each new phrase you made in **C** in a sentence of your own.

Writing a poem for performance

Write your own train poem for performance.

Brainstorming

● What sort of train is it? Who, or what, will be travelling on it?

● What places will it pass through? What sights will be seen?

● Where will its journey end?

● How will the train's speed change during the journey?

● What different sounds will it make?

Planning

● Plan your poem with a different verse for each part of the journey.

● Experiment with rhythm to match the speed and sound of the train over the tracks.

● Decide if your poem will rhyme. You might choose to have only one or two verses which rhyme. Two final rhyming lines often help to make a good ending to a poem which otherwise does not rhyme.

Writing, reviewing and editing

● Write a first draft of your poem.

● Read it aloud. How does it sound? Has it got a strong rhythm? Does the rhythm change at suitable parts of the poem?

● How might it be improved to read aloud better?

● Make any corrections to spelling and punctuation.

Preparing for performance

● Mark up your poem for performance.

● Decide which lines will be read by the whole group, a smaller group or a solo voice.

● Think about lines which would be best read quickly or more slowly, softly or more loudly. Make notes to explain this to the readers.

● Choose people to read your poem.

Performance

● Perform your poem to other children.

● Record it as you do so.

● Listen to the recording. Discuss ways of improving the reading.

● Practise your final version of the reading.

● Perform your poem to another class or the rest of the sch

The Borrowers Afield

The Borrowers are little people four or five inches tall. They live out of sight in people's houses, "borrowing" things like food scraps, or a safety pin. In this story Arrietty and her mother and father, Homily and Pod, have left the safety of their home under a kitchen floor to find relations last heard of living in a badger's set. The outside world is a dangerous place for such little people.

"Keep your eyes skinned," Pod went on, as they all moved off along the path. "If you see anything, do as I do – and sharp, mind. We don't want no running every which way. We don't want no screaming."

"I know," said Arrietty irritably, adjusting her pack. She moved ahead as though trying to get out of earshot.

"You *think* you know," called Pod after her, "but you don't know nothing really; you don't know nothing about cover; nor does your mother: cover's a trained job, cover's like –"

There was a rushing clatter and a dropped shadow and a hoarse, harsh cry; and suddenly, there was Pod – along on the path – face to face with a large, black crow.

The bird stared, wickedly, but a little distrustfully, his cramped toes turned in slightly, his great beak just open. Frozen to stillness Pod stared back – something growing in the path, that's what he looked like – a rather peculiar kind of chunky toadstool. The great bird, very curious, turned his head sideways and tried Pod with his other eye. Pod, motionless, stared back. The crow made a murmur in its throat – a tiny bleat – and, puzzled, it moved forward. Pod let it come, a couple of sideways steps, and then – out of a still face – he spoke: "Get back to where you was," he said evenly, almost conversationally, and the bird seemed to hesitate. "We don't want no nonsense from you," Pod went on steadily, "pigeon-toed, that's what you are! Crows is pigeon-toed, first time it struck me. Staring away like that, with one eye, and your head turned

sideways ... think it pretty, no doubt" – Pod spoke quite pleasantly – "but it ain't, not with *that* kind of beak ..."

The bird became still, its expression no longer curious: there was stark amazement in every line of its rigid body and, in its eye, a kind of ghastly disbelief. "Go on! Get off with you!" shouted Pod suddenly, moving towards it. "Shooo ...!" And, with a distraught glance and panic-stricken croak, the great bird flapped away. Pod wiped his brow with his sleeve as Homily, white-faced and still trembling, crawled out from under a foxglove leaf. "Oh Pod," she gasped, "you were brave – you were wonderful!"

"It's nothing," said Pod, "it's a question of keeping your nerve."

"But the size of it!" said Homily. "You'd never think seeing them flying they was that size!"

"Size is nothing," said Pod, "it's the talk that gets them."

From *The Borrowers Afield*
by **Mary Norton**

Day 1 The big bird

Read the passage, then answer each question.

A Choose the answer which tells what the story really says.
1. The bird which threatened Pod was:
   a) a crow b) a pigeon c) an eagle d) a magpie.
2. When the bird landed it was:
   a) behind Arrietty   b) behind Pod
   c) between Pod and the others
   d) looking sideways at Arrietty.
3. When the bird first looked at him, Pod:
   a) looked like something growing in the path
   b) gave a harsh cry
   c) turned his head sideways
   d) stared at the bird wickedly.
4. Pod survived because:
   a) he kept his nerve   b) he talked to the bird
   c) he frightened it away d) all of the above.
5. Homily was the name of:
   a) Pod's daughter   b) Pod's wife
   c) a big black bird   d) none of the above.

B Answer in complete sentences.
1. Explain in your own words how Pod dealt with the bird.
2. What might have happened if he had attempted to run off?
3. Pick out two examples of non-standard English in the text.
4. Rewrite the examples as standard English.
5. Why do you think the writer uses non-standard English?

C Answer in more than one sentence.

What kind of person do you think Pod is? What makes you think so?

Day 2 Clauses

A Copy these sentences.
Underline the **main clause**.
1. As they all moved off along the path, Pod gave them a warning.
2. Arrietty moved ahead, as though trying to get out of earshot.
3. The bird stared wickedly, his cramped toes turned in slightly.
4. Standing motionless, Pod stared back.
5. He shouted suddenly, moving towards it as he did so.

B Extend these sentences by adding a suitable **clause** of your own.
1. This is Pod.
2. We ate the meal.
3. They arrived at a house.
4. They sat down for a rest.
5. I will buy you a new coat.

C Combine each set of three sentences into **one sentence.**
1. I have enough money. I will buy some plants. I will make a beautiful garden.
2. You are ready. I will bring the car. I will take you into town.
3. He got up. He put on a pair of jeans. They were torn at the knee.
4. He climbed over the stile. He went into a field. The field was by the river.
5. He jammed on the brakes suddenly. He was flung over the handlebars. He landed in the ditch.

D Write five sentences of your own, with at least **two clauses.**

Continuing the story

Write the next chapter in the story of Pod, Homily and Arrietty. What will happen next? Where will they take shelter for the night? How will they try to make sure no other creature attacks them? What might happen if something does?

● Write in the style of the author.

● Use non-standard English for the spoken words of the Borrowers.

● Plan your chapter so that it ends with an exciting event.

Day 5

Adapting writing for a younger audience

The text of *The Borrowers Afield* on page 94 is not suitable for children of five or six to read. There are too many difficult words, and some of the sentences are too long.

Write a new version of the text, especially for children of that age.

● Keep most of your sentences short.

● Use words the children will understand.

● Use standard English for the spoken words.

When you have finished your story, draw some pictures for your younger audience to enjoy.

Read your story to a small group of young children, sharing the pictures with them as you do so.